Cravings

Also by Jyl Lynn Felman

Hot Chicken Wings

Jyl Lynn Felman

CRAVINGS

A Sensual Memoir

BEACON PRESS
BOSTON

Beacon Press
25 Beacon Street
Boston, Massachusetts 02108-2892

Beacon Press books
are published under the auspices of
the Unitarian Universalist Association
of Congregations.

03 02 01 00 99 98 97   8 7 6 5 4 3 2 1

Text design by Elizabeth Elsas
Composition by Wilsted & Taylor Publishing Services

Library of Congress Cataloging-in-Publication Data
Felman, Jyl Lynn, 1954–
    Cravings : a sensual memoir / Jyl Lynn Felman.
      p.   cm.
    ISBN 0-8070-7074-2 (cloth)
    1. Felman, Jyl Lynn, 1954– —Biography. 2. Women
authors, American—20th century—Biography. 3. Jewish
women—United States—Biography.   I. Title.
PS3556.E47255Z465   1997
813'.54—dc21
  [B]   97-10489

FOR MY MOTHER,

EDITH JEANNE (MAYER) FELMAN

1927–1993

When I dare to be powerful—
to use my strength in the service of my vision,
then it becomes less and less important
whether I am afraid.

AUDRE LORDE

Contents

Inventory

I

MY FATHER, MARVIN, in Dayton, Ohio, ships to me, in Northampton, Massachusetts, two huge U-Haul boxes, six orange crushed-velvet chairs, and one hand-painted art deco sea-green-and-ivory European letter-writing desk with a matching green-and-gold-striped chair. They arrive at dusk. It is December and the boxes are freezing next to the woodpile in my garage. Immediately I cover each box with a heavy, navy blue, one-hundred-percent wool American Airlines blanket. But I don't open them. For over an hour, while the sun sets and it gets really cold in my garage, I sit on one of the orange crushed-velvet chairs. For over a year I am unable to open the boxes my father sends me.

Every morning, I go out to the garage and stand directly in front of the boxes, imagining what's packed inside. I stand there drinking my black coffee until I get tired standing. Then I sit down on one of the orange crushed-velvet chairs. It's very soft, sitting on velvet. I imagine my mother sleeping soundly in one of those boxes, tucked in between lots of newsprint so none of her bones break. Her hair is Scotch taped in place. That's how she sleeps, with the tape sticking right on her cheeks, holding her side curls down and imprinting bright red marks on her face all night long while she dreams. The next day, when she brushes her teeth first thing in the morning, not a single hair is out of place. Ever. She has insomnia her entire life.

My mother is a small woman, barely five feet tall. Curled up into a little ball, she easily fits inside one of the boxes. I wonder if my father remembers to tuck her in and pull the newspaper all the way up to her chin. That's how she likes to sleep. Warm and tucked in tight; she has bad circulation. Her hands and feet are cold all the time. I feel my mother resting comfortably right inside with her face turned to the left on her favorite foam rubber pillow. She sleeps soundly for the first time in years. She adores one-hundred-percent silk sheets and pillowcases—cream colored. Marvin doesn't like to sleep on silk; it makes him sweat. My mother waits for me to tap lightly on the outside of the box to let her know I'm here in the garage watching over her.

Judy, my oldest sister, doesn't open her two boxes either. Only she doesn't have a garage, so she pays twenty-five dollars a month to put them in storage. But our middle sister, Jan, opens hers. Immediately. In our own way, we are obsessed about the boxes just as our entire lives we are obsessed about our extremely French Jewish mother. From the very beginning all three daughters want her to ourselves. It's not jealousy that propels us but rather a gnawing, aching hunger that's present at birth and doesn't ever go away, no matter how much food is on the table. Judy Elaine, Jan Ellen, and Jyl Lynn want Edith Jeanne to see them, separate and apart.

When we are growing up, for the first nine years of my life (I am the youngest), my mother buys three of every item of clothing and dresses all her girls identically. She thinks it's cute, pretending that we are a single set of matching triplets. Even though each daughter is two and a half years apart and definitely not identical in personality, shape, or size. We are set up from the start. Not to like each other. I have a photograph of us all dressed in black dresses from Denmark, where the whole country wore the yellow Star of David as a sign of solidarity. Like one big family. The black Danish dresses button down the front and have red sashes tied in back. We look très genteel. Judy and Jan end up modeling for Rike's department store. For ten dollars an hour. I'm a butterball, too little and too round to be a model. I'm two and a half and still a baby.

In the photograph on my desk, Edith holds me tightly to her breasts; I clasp my hands around my mother's neck. We cling fiercely to each other, while Judy and Jan sit poised on either side, crossing their legs at the knee, in the exact pose she teaches us over and over again. My sisters and I pose continuously. For Edith, Marvin, two sets of grandparents, and all *goyim* everywhere. When we are little we learn how to be grown-up. Ladies. We walk clear across the proscenium and back again, our adolescent female bodies totally erect, with the Encyclopedia Britannica on our heads. Edith is afraid that if she doesn't protect us we'll develop curvature of the spine. We develop perfect posture. As the years go by, we become more Chekovian in nature. My father's father is from Russia.

Two years after my mother dies, Marvin divides everything up—by himself. He has UPS deliver to each Felman girl two big, identical brown U-Haul boxes of Edith's "things." And some miscellaneous furniture. He wants to be fair. Jan wants my mother's French hand-carved dark stained-wood love seat. There is only one. I don't even try for the love seat. After all, I get the art deco letter-writing desk from Europe. Jan deserves the love seat and she gets it. Marvin is upset but we absolutely don't want Edith's clothes, which are all matching sets: a blue-and-red leather skirt like the American flag with a Harvé Benard white purl-knit sweater. Edith is into themes. Her taste is impeccable. But no one else can ever possibly wear exactly what she wears: green suede gloves, pumps with light gray sparkling nylons, and a silk scarf, all blended perfectly to go with a royal-blue-and-green speckled wool suit. Each season she has her colors. We aren't allowed to wear white (or even ivory) a single minute *before* Memorial

Day or an hour *after* Labor Day. White is the shortest season of all.

Marvin doesn't understand that we cannot wear our mother's clothes. So he keeps them hanging in the closet for over two years; the shape of his wife's body is completely visible. She has her own Eau de London smell that lingers on her clothes for months after she dies. We girls have our own individual aesthetic, which we work hard to develop. It's difficult and requires a lot of self-confidence to carve out an identifiable style separate and apart from Edith's. To our father's great dismay, we refuse her small private collection of designer handbags. We have to. She has them in all colors—black patent leather, multicolored beaded—and in all shapes and sizes—square, rectangle, round, oval, and pillbox style à la Jackie Kennedy with a matching velvet pillbox hat—arranged neatly on the shelves in their bedroom.

It's a completely awkward situation. Refusing Edith's clothes and accessories. She does have a marvelous collection of bathrobes. I decide to keep the Chinese maroon silk robe with the salmon-colored pelican wings printed on the sleeves. She never wears it because she doesn't want to spill anything on the maroon silk that won't come out. Chinese silk has to be dry cleaned—delicately. I don't wear it either. Black coffee ruins silk. Marvin is afraid none of his girls will ever talk to him again after we open the boxes. Silences are a big Felman thing.

Passed down from one generation to the next. The silences go on forever. My father's father from Russia doesn't talk to his first born-in-America daughter. And she doesn't talk to him. For his entire life Marvin, the baby, is caught in the middle. Only he'll never admit it. He says he loves them both equally. But he doesn't invite his only sister, our aunt, to our mother's funeral because he doesn't want to upset his father. I understand. But how can he really expect us to get along? My mother says that Shirley, her only sister, is her best friend. But Marvin and Aunt Shirley don't talk to each other. That's why it takes him so long to clean out the apartment. He is afraid of all the silences.

I have the great idea that we should write down on a small file card in order of our preference the three items that we most want and send the short list to Marvin without saying a word to each other about what we write down. In this particular way, we are like my mother's favorite Southern Jewish woman playwright, Lillian Hellman, and her play *The Little Foxes*. Related and relentless. Forever. This is serious. And occupies us for an entire lifetime. Ultimately it is Marvin who makes the final decision. He wants to be ethical in his decision-making, à la King Solomon and the fake mother but real baby boy the king was going to cut in half so the real mother would reveal herself. The king's plan worked. According to my plan each daughter/sister is supposed to get at least one item out of her top three choices. That's where the three comes from. Marvin and I both think this is a good idea for dividing up Edith's possessions.

Edith loves all children everywhere and wants more, but after three girls in a row Marvin has enough. We run around the house naked all the time. Only Marvin keeps all his clothes on. He's slightly inhibited around us, his three girls. And Edith. He makes absolutely sure we know how to play softball, throw a football, and shoot baskets hitting the backboard in the center directly above the hoop so the ball just drops in. Whether we want to or not. Judy hates sports. Marvin pays Jan a dollar for every softball she catches. I am a natural-born athlete. Edith's favorite sport is bowling. She wins many championships on the Hadassah team and keeps all her trophies on display in the basement next to the atomic bomb shelter. I love to jog but Marvin says this is bad for women of childbearing years.

We speak often about the situation, me in Massachusetts, Marvin in Ohio, as if we are an old married couple. I know this is how my parents used to talk, before my mother stops talking. They talk about everything. Except my father's father, Dave, and my mother's mother, Tessie, who never like each other. Those two are off-limits for discussion. My mother is my father's best friend until she is fifty years old and is diagnosed with Parkinson's. And then my mother doesn't want to be friends with anybody any more, not just Marvin. My mother doesn't want the three Js fighting over her. "One day, when your father and I are long gone, you girls will be all that's left." She tells me this all the time when I am growing up. "Whatever you do, don't fight with your sisters. I want you girls to be best friends."

Making our own lists seems fair to me, since by the time she dies we all want the exact same thing. Judy and Jan don't think there is anything fair about listing three items on a file card and sending it to Marvin. We never stop fighting over our mother. After she's dead we stop speaking to each other. For years at a time until the isolation is much more familiar than the family itself. And we truly are Lillian Hellman's keen little foxes.

Jews have been lost to each other for centuries: across the Balkans, in the Gulag Archipelago, in Ethiopia, and most recently in the villages of Cochin, India. But it hurts, this family "blood is thicker than water" separation. My father's father is an orphan and so is his wife. After a long journey, my grandparents land at Ellis Island all alone in one big boat with a lot of Jews they don't know. They disembark and wander around the dock, waiting for relatives who sign all the proper papers but never show up. Then they find each other, become my Bubbe and Zadie, and never, ever let go. Until my grandmother Eva dies. And my grandfather and the rabbi have a huge fight about the meaning of death in Judaism. My grandfather slams the front door shut and never talks to the rabbi again. This is unfortunate because the rabbi is a dear friend of my mother's and a very famous man.

Waking up in the morning I feel odd; I know this

is not the American way. Families are supposed to get along; Jewish families especially are supposed to be there for each other. All the time. Including times of great need. Because we are a people abandoned by most of the world. That's why the State of Israel made the Law of Return. And the rest of the world eagerly agreed. That the Jews can and should return to Jerusalem automatically, whenever they want, as fast as they can. All they have to do is agree to leave their mother country behind. For good. In the beginning, I never want the silverware; I don't cook. But by the end, all of us want Edith's silverware with the letter "F" for fish engraved on each utensil. Fish is my mother's mother's maiden name. Years later, when my mother marries my father, "F" for Fish naturally becomes "F" for Felman. The transition is smooth. It's as if Edith always knew she had to marry someone whose last name began with an "F" because of the silverware. She begins her search as soon as she graduates high school in June and starts her first semester at Ohio State the following September. The search ends when she is nineteen. Two semesters later. She finds Marvin at Chi Epsilon Chi, the only Jewish fraternity on campus, and gets him to agree to ask her to marry him. Tessie, her French mother, isn't ecstatic about parking lots, Ashkenazi Russian Jews, or marriage to Marvin. Both my parents have inferiority complexes. No one tells me so directly. I just sense it. After all, the French abandoned Dreyfus for years on that horrible Devil's Island. And the whole South stood by and watched as Leo Frank was attacked by a furious mob.

The silverware is a six-piece set with a salad, main course, and dessert fork, one knife with slightly serrated edges sharp enough to cut a kosher veal chop or slice an Empire chicken breast in half, plus a standard-size teaspoon and a very wide soup spoon that was ethnically and culturally designed to be round enough to hold a whole matzo ball or pick up two kreplach in one dunk. There are settings for six. My mother's silverware is unique; this particular style was popular before the war and wasn't made in America, so replacement pieces are impossible to obtain. Unless the owner pays for an overseas search, like the advertisement in the *New York Times* for hard-to-locate silver or lost family relatives. Specifically Jewish searches for personal effects and people become popular in the late '50s and early '60s.

These searches are still going on today, with whole governments becoming involved across international lines. It's a repayment plan. But the entire family has to agree to the settlement before it can be finalized. Jan suggests that we each get two place settings. She thinks this is fair. I don't. I don't know what Judy thinks. She refuses to tell either of us. Jan's other idea is to divide the silverware up by category. She wants the forks. They are unusually long stemmed and the prongs are excellent for eating grilled Atlantic salmon with fresh pesto and basil or fillet of gray sole lightly dipped in an egg and flour batter and sautéed in slivered almonds.

Three years before Edith dies, Jan calls to tell me that she should get the silverware because she and her husband, Myron, entertain a lot. They are desperate for the extra place settings. She reminds me that Judy is anorectic and hasn't eaten much for the last fifteen years. She explains softly over the phone that I just don't need a whole set of silverware all to myself. I never say a word in response. I can have anything else I want, but she would really appreciate the silverware. It would mean a lot to her. And Myron. Besides, she'd like to keep it in the family. And I don't have any children. Every few months, Jan brings up the silverware in the middle of a phone conversation about our mother's illness. Slowly, almost imperceptibly, I begin to want the silverware myself. All six place settings.

It becomes a mad craving. Every time I pick up a fork or a soup spoon, I imagine how much better the food would taste. Especially the leftover challah French toast with orange slices, scooped up at the end of Edith's fork with the specially engraved letter "F" and placed lovingly into my mouth. If only I were eating with Edith's sterling silver fork. My mother feeds me. Like when I am a baby. In my fantasy she never stops feeding me, not even when I grow up, temporarily stop shaving my legs, use a menstrual sponge from the floor of the Atlantic instead of a Kotex tampon, cut off all my hair above my ears, and major in creative writing at Syracuse University. (Jan went to Emory.) Storytelling, like arguing with G-d, is a big part of Jewish tradition. I thought my parents would be pleased that I want to keep the family stories alive. Historically, Jews thrive on retrieving lost memory.

Staring at the boxes in my garage, I feel sure Marvin gave me the entire set of silverware. After all, I am the baby and the most like Edith. I set a beautiful *Shabbos* table. With deep pink alstroemerias cut short and placed in the center, next to the hand-made ceramic *kiddish* cup. Judy and Jan don't observe the Sabbath. Although Myron, Jan's husband, went to *heder* just like Marvin when he was growing up. The young men could have studied together. They're both extremely competitive. I light my candles every Friday night. And say all the blessings. I also celebrate Tu b'Shevat, the tree holiday. It's a modern festival, Edith's favorite. Every February, until she's too sick and they have to move out of the house on Lynn Avenue and into the apartment downtown, she plants a new hawthorn tree, with red berries, in the backyard. We watch the berries grow from the breakfast nook. And I always remember to mourn the destruction of the second temple on Tishah B'av. It's a summer holiday coming after Shavuot, when, after a very long wait, we finally receive the Ten Commandments and become a moral people.

Jan already has everything: a handsome, intelligent, wealthy husband who plays a mean game of tennis, and once in a while when they see each other he even beats Marvin; a beautiful and brilliant young son who plays chess, speaks Hebrew and French, and is a superb athlete, excelling in soccer. The Felman-Katzes live in a magnificent home that contains fantastic art. My middle sister has great taste. She's a lawyer and plays the flute. Chopin. Bach. She even plays along with Jean-Pierre Rampal when he's on the radio. When we are growing up, she has to practice her scales all alone in the basement with the soundproof door shut tight because I am busy practicing on the baby grand Steinway in the middle of the living room at the same time. The house just isn't big enough for both of us. *Für Elise* fills the whole house for hours. Judy has no musical ability.

Jan, like Edith, is an excellent cook. Everything. From scratch. Appetizers: stuffed mushrooms with feta and Gruyère, chopped walnuts, fresh spinach, and sautéed-in-butter shallots. Or dessert: three-layer strawberry meringue, Swiss chocolate, and hazelnut filling, baked in a hot oven at 425 degrees in a home-made, all-butter piecrust. Neither Judy nor I know how to cook. Jan's whole family is well rounded and fits into the American scene well. Unlike Judy who is divorced and me who's been a lesbian for twenty years, our middle sister actually has a family all to herself: one husband, a single child, and a recently acquired dog, a small, miniature black poodle. Which is highly unusual since Edith doesn't like pets of any kind. They smell and require a lot of attention. Judy has to keep her hamsters in the garage, which is freezing. Myron tells me that after a couple of short weeks, Jan and the poodle really bond. So the decision about the silverware is really just between Judy and me. That's the way I see the situation.

Instead of following the rules as Marvin lays them out in a letter, Jan makes her own itemized list. As though she is preparing for a Sotheby auction, she spends a day in my parents' apartment in Ohio numbering and tagging everything in sight with masking tape. The taping and tagging take over eight hours. She sends a photocopy of the completed list to Marvin, Judy, and me. So we can study it. The list is very long. I can hardly read her handwriting. It's small and tight. She's pleased. And genuinely thinks she has simplified the task for us all. Reduced the stress in the equitable distribution of our mother's meager personal property. She even calls me ahead of time, singing into my tape machine, to tell me the list is on its way. After receiving her handwritten, three-page list with a brief note attached, I don't return her calls or speak to her for months.

In high school Jan stops speaking to me. She turns her head away at home and in the hallway of Fairview High School whenever I pass her on the way to the bathroom. It's awful. Hysterical, I beg Edith to intervene. She is humiliated that her daughters are behaving this way. Family is all there is. She taught us better, she reminds me. My middle sister, Jan, stops speaking to me in tenth grade because I make the varsity cheerleading squad and get a new navy blue V-neck wool sweater with a big "F" embroidered in the middle, and she has to be a Scotchette like Judy. But Jan is a National Merit Scholar finalist and knows all the answers on *Jeopardy*, which neither Judy nor I ever do.

Because we fight over her things, Marvin thinks Edith's girls are immature and ungrateful. This is also what his father thinks. My father doesn't understand that this is a very old fight. Biblical in nature. With such deep resonances. After all, Jacob, with the help of his beloved mother, stole his older brother Esau's birthright. Right out from under him. The father, Isaac, dies distraught at the deception. The whole family never recovers from this small act of childish betrayal. I don't know what to do. The fight goes on and on, until it has a life of its own. I keep rereading Jan's letter, looking for clues. All my life, I want to understand. Edith and Marvin. My two sisters. The Felmans. The long-term effect of the long journey from the old country to the new one. Including the subsequent life in the Diaspora.

My parents never make it to France before my mother dies. It starts with the headaches that she thinks are massive brain tumors. She lies on the couch for hours at a time with her right arm covering her forehead. For two whole years I am the only one at home. Finally, I have her all to myself. The other two Js are off at college. Together, Edith, Marvin, and I rebuild the family; we become a team. Drinking black coffee in the morning and listening to Barbara Walters on the *Today* show on TV. We share equally the *Dayton Daily News*—the front page, Living Section, and Sports centerfold. The *New York Times* is delivered early Sunday morning. Which we also share equally. There's no fighting as long as each section is folded perfectly back in place. I even forget I have two older sisters. No one mentions them at mealtime. All through high school, I hear her moan softly into the living room while I practice *Für Elise*. Over and over again. I keep getting confused. The chords stick together as she moans.

Ten years later, when I am twenty-six, she's finally diagnosed. She dies ten days before my thirty-ninth birthday. I'm Pisces and so is my first girlfriend, Shoshana, very creative and extremely sensitive. Marvin, Edith, and Jan are all born in October. In my family, and my tribe, letter writing is a powerful means of communication. All over Europe, for centuries, Jews are the scribes of the royal court. We're also the People of the Book. Important details are written down. And then passed from generation to generation. That's how I find out that my oldest sister, Judy, whose birthday is in April, is married. And that Jan is pregnant with her only child, Aaron. In the letter she writes that she's not planning to tell our mother and father until the baby is born. She doesn't want overinvolved grandparents. Everyone writes to everyone. Especially when no one is talking to anyone. It's a way of maintaining the connection. For years, I save all the letters I receive from every member of my family.

Dear Jyl,

I wanted you to have a copy of this—
Feel free to telephone to discuss—

Love, Jan

The three-page list is addressed to Marvin and dated two whole days earlier than the note to me:

Dear Dad,

It was a pleasure spending time with you this weekend. Thank-you for being so hospitable.

I've given a great deal of thought to the divisions of Mother's things. In particular, I have appreciated the importance you put on the three of us not feeling there is any inequality.

While I feel I could make a case why I should get certain items, I suppose my sisters could do the same.

To avoid such potential wrangling, I think each of us should have an equal share of anything we want. If 3 of us want the silver, then we each would get an equal share of it. If 3 of us want the gold rimmed flowered dishes, then they should be divided 3 ways.

After the distribution we could choose to add to any partial collection (as you & Edith did with the china) and/or trade among ourselves.

Since many of the things have such strong emotional value to each of us, I think this is the only way to keep peace and assist you in avoiding partiality.

I telephoned Judy & Jyl to discuss these things. As they have not yet returned my call, I have sent them each a copy of this letter.

The things I want follow—

Take care. Looking forward to talking with you soon.

Love, Jan

The inventory follows the letter:

LIST

1. Gold rimmed flowered French China (Limoges & other China, French).
2. Silver Flatware & serving pieces with JAN marked on them.
3. Silver serving dishes and trays with JAN marked on (& plates).
4. Rhine Glasses.
5. Linens in bureau in Master Bedroom with JAN marked.
6. Cut glasses w/JAN on it.
7. Slipper chair from Master Bedroom.
8. Framed Family photos hanging on walls throughout.
9. Oil picture of girl playing flute plus Dali prints.
10. Hanging needlepoint (especially Aunt Shirley's).

11. Oil portraits of me & my two sisters if they don't
    want it.
12. Needlepoint chair in 2nd bedroom.
13. Photo Albums as marked with JAN (will make
    copies for my two sisters—if they desire).
14. Silver candlesticks in box in Master Bedroom.
15. Silver wine glasses.
16. Crystal glasses.

II

Upon receiving Jan's list, my oldest sister Judy writes
Jan a letter and sends a copy to Marvin and me:

Dear Jan,

Thank you for sending me a complete list of all the
things of Mother's that you want. Although I left you a
message that I received the letter, I wanted to respond
in a like manner, in writing, and I'm sending both Dad
and Jyl a copy also.

It will take me time to respond and I will want to
go to Dayton, too, and go through Mother's "special"
things myself. Before submitting my complete list to
Dad.

Love, Judy

I don't write a list or a letter. But I am afraid I'll get
left out of the final distribution altogether and end up

with just Edith's leftovers. I know Edith wouldn't want that to happen. I call my father, hysterical. He says not to worry, he'll take care of it, and that he's the one in charge of dividing everything up in the end. When my two boxes arrive, I take the letter with me out to the garage dressed in the lime green parka my mother sent me fifteen years ago, before she got sick. I stare at the U-Haul boxes imagining my mother waking up inside, her hair perfectly in place. I feel her raging; my hands shake. I know we aren't supposed to fight over things. Things can always be replaced. I read out loud to my dead mother. It's people who are irreplaceable. Even little Anne Frank knew that. And told everyone in that journal of hers, which she kept daily for two years while she lived in a dark, windowless attic without fresh water or enough air.

Edith always reads out loud to me. At night before I fall asleep. She teaches at Hillel Academy, the first Jewish day school in Dayton, Ohio, and always reads out loud to her third-grade class. They are perfect, giving Mrs. Felman *The Favorite Teacher Award* three years in a row, until all the other teachers from Israel and Russia feel completely unappreciated and the principal has to put a stop to the award. My mother is theatrical; she plays Dorothy in *The Wizard of Oz* in the Fairview elementary school play. For three nights in a row she receives a standing ovation. From the front row all the way to the last seat in the balcony.

We sit in the balcony, in the last row, when my

mother takes all the girls and not Marvin downtown to Memorial Hall to see *The Sound of Music* when it finally comes to the Midwest. Marvin doesn't like universal themes. He thinks it's the particulars that ultimately make the difference. Edith disagrees. She sings along with Maria Von Trapp. And points out how congenial all the Von Trapp children are, how well they get along. Brothers and sisters. Boys and girls. All the Von Trapps dress in identical brown leather pedal pushers, white cotton shirts with suspenders, and white knee socks with little black tassels. Edith thinks it's so cute. The hills are completely alive, filled with the sound of music and children's voices. I can't sing and neither can my sisters.

On stage, in *The Wizard of Oz*, my mother closes her eyes. Shaking her small head, which is covered in long, black braids of thick Scandinavian yarn, Edith clicks her heels together three times and says, "There's no place like home." All my life I want to believe her. The Jews wander forty years in the desert looking for home. And just when they get really comfortable, blending in, putting down roots on a good piece of real estate, they have to flee in the middle of the night or be killed. Only the borders are closed and all the German shepherds are barking really loud. Terrified, the Jews are forced to turn back. In preparation for the future, on alternating weeks, all the Felman girls take ice skating at the big rink at Icelandia and elocution lessons on the off week from Mrs. Shiloh. We're very busy girls. It's good practice, my mother-Dorothy-from-Kansas says. "Good diction is part of good style." Mrs. Lee Jewel is our ice-skating coach; the whole family, including Marvin, skates together on Sunday afternoons. "Good style is a necessary part of a Jewish girl's repertoire." My mother tells me to be careful, because I am born with a lot of savoir faire and it's tricky living in the Diaspora with all that know-how. "But, unlike your sisters, who had to acquire theirs over time, you just came out that way."

We, my sisters and I, are treated exactly the same with a few minor exceptions. Which all of us remember in exact detail. Judy has to go to Ohio State, while Jan and I are allowed to pick the college of our choice. I am allowed to pierce my ears before Jan is, even though I am two-and-a-half years younger and to defile the human body is against the Talmud. Jan doesn't learn to drive until she is thirty-five. When she does, no one in the family wants to ride with her. Judy flunks her test three times in a row—not the written exam but the driving part. We're not allowed to mention it. Ever. Even as a joke. I pass both the written test and the road test. The first time. As soon as I turn sixteen.

"But I told your father immediately. That you were different. I could tell by the way you curled yourself up into a little ball until I fed you. You were hungry. All the time." Moses told the Israelites not to take more manna from Heaven than they could eat at one meal. They didn't listen. Even though plenty of manna fell from Heaven for breakfast the very next day. "I was afraid

you were going to grow up fat and have a weight problem your whole life. I don't know why, but you always
wanted more." My mother weighs one hundred and
five pounds her entire life, except when she is pregnant
with each of us. She can eat anything. Even sitting for
years in a wheelchair, she has fast metabolism. She
doesn't gain a single pound until the very end. When
her stomach starts protruding only slightly. But I don't
say a word. Unlike Judy, Jan, and Jyl, who have to be
vigilant about what we put in our mouths our whole life.
When I am born I weigh nine-and-a-half pounds. I am
a heavy baby for a short woman to carry. Both my sisters
weigh just under seven pounds. The perfect weight for
newborn Jewish females. Edith ate more with me. Together, we are very hungry. And can't stop eating. Judy
and Jan call me piglet when we are growing up. Pigs are
hoofed creatures and eat anything that's placed on the
ground in front of them. They aren't kosher and my sisters know it. They're scavengers. They smell.

Slowly, I begin to read out loud to my mother in the
garage, sitting comfortably on her orange crushed-
velvet chair. I look up at the two U-Haul boxes covered
with the navy blue American Airline blankets. When I
get cold, I take one of the wool blankets and wrap my
legs up tight. Just like she taught me, I make sure my
feet are covered. Then I keep reading. The attached
note is dated French style, with the day first and the
month, May, in the middle: 31.5.95. All the family put
the day ahead of the month. Except Marvin. And his

father, who do it the American way. Jews in general follow the lunar calendar, which is just a reflection of the
wonderful and mysterious cycles of the moon. That's
why we're never sure from year to year exactly when the
holidays are. Gentiles don't understand. According to
the Gregorian calendar cycle, which follows the sun,
their holidays come at the same time every year, on the
exact same day. There are never any surprises.

My mother tries to give me her wedding ring when
I'm visiting her, right before she gets really sick. For a
long time I want something of hers to call my own. But
when she offers me her ring, I'm upset. I don't wear
rings. I'm a lesbian. I give it back without even trying it
on. My left fourth finger is the exact same size in diame-
ter as my mother's. I think my mother is asking me to
marry her. Months later, drinking my black coffee, I realize I made a huge mistake. I don't ever want to know
who gets her wedding ring. Shaking my head no, I say,
"Give me something I'll wear." Edith is stunned. Hurt.
And so am I. How could we miss each other so much?

III

Right before their fortieth wedding anniversary, my father prepares to move my mother out of the house I
grew up in. I am home to say good-bye to Lynn Avenue
and the house when Edith gives me her wedding album. "Out of all the girls, you'll take good care of the

pictures. You won't let anything happen to them. I know the pictures mean a lot to you." It's a beautiful album with a clear Lucite cover with my mother, the beautiful young bride, shining through in her long, white pearl dress. She's not exactly smiling; she's posing. Just like she taught us. With her right foot slightly in front of her left. Her wedding bouquet is small. Miniature white roses. Much smaller than I imagine. My mother loves flowers. I love the album. Both sets of grandparents are in there, on either side of the next generation, the new bride and groom. The old country and the new world. The wedding is in Wheeling, West Virginia, where Edie is born. The reception is in Tessie's backyard. Aunt Shirley is there without a date. She hasn't met her future husband, Uncle Nathen, yet. She wears thick, black-rimmed glasses that afterwards, when she sees the pictures, Tessie immediately throws away.

Marvin looks exceptionally young, almost as if it's his Bar Mitzvah instead of his wedding. He wears a black silk yarmulke on the back of his head. They cut the cake together. I can't see my mother's wedding ring in the photo. My father's hand is on top of hers as they slice gently through the white almond marzipan filling, which is very expensive in those days. My grandfather from Russia prefers plain yellow honey cake, but it's a wedding, his only son's big *simcha*, not Rosh Hashanah. I feel like I really got something special. That I am special, finally, when my mother gives me her album. So when she asks for it back a month later, I'm hysterical. I don't understand. I thought she gave it to me. To keep. Forever. How could she want it back? I write Aunt Shirley a letter explaining what's going on with her big sister. And ask her to intervene, please. Aunt Shirley calls Edith and they discuss it. My mother writes me to say that she just wants to borrow the album back for a little bit. Then I can have it. For good.

I think Judy and Jan find out that she gave me the pictures. And they're mad and have stopped speaking to Edith. That's why there's all this trouble now. I refuse. The pictures are all mine and she can't have them back. We begin a long fight over my mother's wedding album, which she gives me forever and then wants back. She just wants to look at a few of the pictures. Of her parents, Tessie and Al. And of my father, who is so young and handsome. One more time. I don't believe her. I tell her I'll make copies for everyone. As many as she wants, but it's mine. It's unethical to take back what she gave me. The Talmud says *to give with an open heart. And then the giver must let go.* We never resolve the photo album crisis before she dies. The Talmud also says *to give anonymously is the highest form of giving.* This is one of Edith's favorite sayings. The other one is *A soft answer turneth away wrath.* Which before her marriage to Marvin she single-handedly embroidered in red and black thread. And then framed and hung above the kitchen stove.

IV

Edith gives me one last present. To assuage our difficult situation, I think. A bracelet that I admire from the moment my father gives it to her. Only by the time she gives it to me, she's really sick and is barely talking at all to anyone. Moaning, she has the nurse unclasp the bracelet from her swollen wrist. Then with her fist, she shoves it over to me across the kitchen table. No one in the family knows that she gives me her solid gold diamond bracelet. Each link is a tiny little heart. All the hearts are connected to each other. The diamonds sit in the middle of each heart link. She doesn't tell anyone, and neither do I. After she dies, my father says my mother's bracelet is missing. He doesn't want to accuse anyone, but he thinks the nurse may have slipped it into her purse one day. Without thinking. I think Judy took it.

At first I don't understand that he's talking about the bracelet he gave Edith and she gave me. I feel special. Selected out from the other sisters and seen by my mother when she gives me her favorite bracelet. Even though I don't wear jewelry except large hoop earrings, I wear the gold bracelet. Every day. Our wrists are the exact same size before hers start to swell. I don't know when I realize that the missing bracelet is the one my mother gives me without telling anyone. I don't know what to do. I didn't steal it; but no one will believe me. I don't tell anyone that I have the bracelet. Jan wants Marvin to file an insurance claim and Judy tells Marvin that she never trusted those nurses anyway. I take off my mother's bracelet. It doesn't feel like mine any more. Even though she gave it to me. I swear she did.

I put it back in the red satin box it came in and put the box in the back of my dresser. I don't wear Edith's bracelet out in public again. When the U-Haul boxes arrive, Marvin says to me that the only thing still missing is my mother's gold bracelet. He thought for sure that he would find it in the apartment with the rest of her matching jewelry. Sometimes, late at night, I go upstairs and take out the red satin box with my mother's gold bracelet tucked inside. I sit down on my bed, slip it on my thin wrist, and open up the wedding album. That I never make copies of for Judy or Jan. Or Marvin.

I turn the pages, one by one. My mother's posture is perfect. Absolutely. No one would ever guess that her right hip is higher than her left one. By two inches. She has curvature of the spine. And never tells anyone but me how upset she is that her posture is impaired. Her whole life. Tessie couldn't fix it and surgery would only make it worse. Every skirt and dress has to be hemmed longer on the right side. Staring at my mother's wedding picture, I know that good posture is everything.

Cruising

T HERE ARE many things about my family that I do not understand. Like what are we doing in Haiti. When I am fourteen. In 1968, according to the *Encyclopedia Judaica*, there are only fifty Jews left in the whole country. Haiti has never been hospitable to my people. Unlike Jamaica and Cuba, which opened their arms wide. I want to ask Marvin how we get to Port-au-Prince from Dayton, Ohio. It's a long, long way from the Midwest.

Although why we go in August I understand. Completely. August is the only time Marvin leaves Dayton. For three reasons. First: Business is slow at the parking lots. Not many cars to park. Instead of shopping, everyone is swimming at the YMCA or the Jewish Community Center straight out Salem Avenue. Second: Airfares are down. Because. It's too hot to travel. And finally: It's off-season. Excellent package deals are available, especially on the American Plan, which includes three full meals a day from a specially designed menu.

Late summer. Hotels in the sun belt give the staff a vacation. Service is limited. But not on the way to Haiti. There are a lot of big food buffets. Most Jews stay home in August. Except the Felmans, who love the quiet and staying at empty resorts. All by ourselves. As long as there's at least one other couple who play bridge and don't eat pork in front of Marvin, everything's okay. I never learn how to play bridge. Edith says *One day you'll be sorry. That you don't play.* (Judy and Jan both play.) *It's an important skill. To have at your fingertips.* I prefer *Scrabble*. Only not with Marvin. He always makes up new words. That I've never heard of. Like *fez*. Which he swears is a hat.

When I am ten, we take our first full-length family vacation. Which prefigures our Haitian excursion. We go to Miami Beach for ten days. Spread out over two weekends. So Marvin is actually gone only five working days. We fly USAir. The only carrier that offers nonstop jet service out of Dayton. It's hard to leave Dayton on anything other than a very small prop plane. We spread out. Take up an entire row with three seats on one side of the aisle. Prereserved for the girls so there's no fighting about the window. We sit in our birth order. (Edith's idea. From teaching the third grade. She understands. How important it is to be fair. Divide things up equally. Between all the ten-year-olds.) Jan is always in the middle. Even if we sit in reverse birth order. I actually prefer the aisle. I hate to be trapped. I am not claustrophobic.

Edith and Marvin sit across from us. Marvin likes the exit row. There's more leg room. And he can get out faster. Historically, Jews always need an escape route at a moment's notice. We're on our way to the Fontaine-bleau to stay on a high floor in two connecting end rooms. One for Judy, Jan, and Jyl and another one for Edith and Marvin. My father prefers sleeping in his own bed. It's always more comfortable at home. Edith adores sleeping in new, unknown, faraway places. We don't use the connecting door unless there's an emergency in the middle of the night. Edith insists that we keep the door closed but not locked. We use the hall. And always, as if we are at home on Lynn Avenue, when the door is closed we knock first before entering.

The Fontainebleau in Miami Beach is an elegant, old-world French hotel. Decorated in Edith's favorite colors: peach melba and sea green. Heavy satin curtains hang from the ceiling in the lobby. All the way down, until the peach satin skims the top of the green marble floor. To create the positive effect of simple grandeur, gilded mirrors line the walls, side by side. Upon arrival and departure, I wave to myself in the lobby. Both the coffee shop, La Crêpe, and the dining room, L'Au-berge, remain open in August. I have my own favorite corner table by the big picture window. For ten days I look out from La Crêpe at the Atlantic. I drink coffee, order a warm pecan Danish with butter, and read the

Florida Sun Times. I dream that Edith and I are together. Just the two of us. We are in the middle of a very
deep conversation about the meaning of life. Judaism.
And what it means to be female in the twentieth century. Edith says I'm too serious. I spread out, enjoying
the whole table. And my mother. The entire coffee shop
belongs to us. Temporarily.

Earlier in the morning, the maître d' orders crêpes
suzette for Edith and apple blintzes with sour cream
for Marvin. The maître d' at the Fontainebleau understands the Felmans. Better than we understand ourselves. Our eating habits. The first time we arrive in
Miami Beach, my mother is in mourning. For those
three boys who were killed in the South. And left bleed-
ing in shallow graves on the side of the road. Nineteen
sixty-four is an exhausting, but proud year. For the
Jews. Edith identifies with the mothers, Mrs. Good-
man, Mrs. Schwerner, and Mrs. Chaney. She reminds
us that she must die first. Which she does. She absolutely does not want to outlive her children. Judy, Jan,
and Jyl are supposed to say *Kaddish* for her. And not
vice versa. Whenever we travel as a family, Edith has
an entire set of rules that everyone agrees to follow. Or
there's no family vacation.

We must participate, with enthusiasm, in at least
one group activity during the day. Such as Ping-Pong.
Shuffleboard. Water polo. Or bingo. On rainy days, we
are to be available for touring no later than nine A.M.
Art museums. French bakeries. Homemade candy

stores. Judaica shops. The local conservative *shul*. If we ever leave the hotel grounds by ourselves, we leave Edith a note at the front desk. Printed neatly on the hotel stationery. Edith's favorite rule: We must eat dinner together, as a unit. Every night. At seven. And get dressed up. Because we've been loafing all day. For breakfast, lunch, and all snacks in between, we're mostly on our own. And can eat whenever we want. With whomever. Unless Edith wants us all to have brunch. She's found a truly exciting delicatessen that didn't exist last year. Traveling together, we call her "Eager Edie." She's the bus driver.

After four years at the Fontainebleau off-season in hot August, Eager Edie wants to do something extra special. That's how we get to Haiti. The girls are growing up. I'm in eighth grade. Judy and Jan are in high school. Pretty soon we won't be a whole family or a nuclear unit any more. Edith talks about her plans all the time. And passes out brochures with spectacular pictures. Orange and pink sunsets. She has to win Marvin over to her side. Marvin needs a rest. It snows a lot in Dayton.

Most of the winter he is up at 5:00 A.M. plowing the snow into big piles in the corner of the parking lots. Then he has to shovel a clear path for all his customers. By the time August comes around, Marvin is exhausted. All he wants to do is play water polo and bridge. Read a good thick historical novel about the Warsaw Ghetto uprising. And rest in between activities. We go through this every year. Edith wants to travel. See the world. Taste new and exotic dishes that she doesn't have to cook herself. She loves to eat breakfast out. Or in bed. Marvin likes a table. A comfortable chair. The newspaper. A good reading light. At least sixty watts. No glare.

Edith does some research. Her specialty. And we end up in two connecting cabins on the *Queen Victoria*. Cruising smoothly out into the beautiful Atlantic, far away from the dirty, polluted, unsafe, crime-ridden shores of Manhattan. (It takes a good twenty-four hours to clear the pollution.) The food on board is French, kosher style. The sauces are served on the side. Marvin eats only fish that's specially prepared for him. Like when Edith orders kosher meals ahead of time on USAir. On our way to Haiti, we stop to celebrate *Shabbos* in New Rochelle. To eat real lox and bagels, whipped cream cheese with chives, capers, a lemon wedge, and thin-sliced red onions for breakfast with Edith's sister, Shirley, her husband, Nathen, and their three kids. The *Queen Victoria* doesn't serve bagels and cream cheese. There is brioche. And daily, hourly, light fluffy golden warm croissants served with unsalted whipped butter and raspberry preserves or chocolate spread. I love chocolate spread. So does Edith. She likes hers heated.

I don't know how Edith gets Marvin to agree to take his girls out on the Atlantic. She can be persuasive. He finally gets excited saying good-bye to Aunt Shirley and

Cruising

Uncle Nathen at the dock at Port Authority in New York City. Everybody waves good-bye. All the people on the dock wave to all the people on the boat. It feels like one big Purim party. With hats, balloons, crepe paper streamers, and noise makers. Edith is so happy. She loves to visit her only sister, Shirley. To welcome the Sabbath and light candles together. Family is important. And ours is so small. This is a dream come true.

Our first cruise. Meals on the *Queen Victoria* are magnificent. Edith has seen the pictures. Of the huge ice sculptures. That don't ever melt. For the entire trip. Dinner is served at seven sharp. Under a huge, shimmering chandelier. In the King's Dining Room. Our table is preassigned. I hate to eat with strangers. The light from the chandelier is very bright. Judy wears big, black sunglasses. That cover her whole face. For the whole meal. No one says a word. We're used to big, black sunglasses. Jackie Kennedy wore them in public for years after Jack was killed.

The first thing we do as a family on board the *Queen Victoria* is to take a guided-by-Marvin tour of the exact location of the lifeboats. By the time we are two years old, all the Felman girls can swim the crawl alone in the deep end of the Jewish Community Center pool. We've taken the test, received our Red Cross badges, and are all *intermediate* swimmers. Edith thinks that swimming is one of the most important skills a person can have. Survival. *The earlier you learn, the better.* Marvin-the-guide has us practice putting on our life jackets. They're huge, puffy, and orange. He times us. With the second hand on his Timex. We have to get the puffy orange jackets on in under five minutes.

I am not having fun. Marvin wins. I observe my father. I can tell. The exact moment he wishes. Privately to himself. That he had three boys—Jonathan, Jacob, and Joshua—to play with instead of us, his three girls. Plus Edith. Who is his number one, best playmate. We haven't even unpacked, we're so busy. In our tiny connecting cabins. Judy, Jan, and I have to sleep together. We flip a coin to see who gets the rollaway bed. Just because I'm the baby doesn't mean I can't sleep in a real bed. We flip. Marvin's quarter. I win two out of three. Heads.

I pick the top bunk. I need as much privacy as possible. Edith thinks it will be absolutely wonderful to look out and not see dry land. For days. I think it's going to be a long trip. My mother says I'll fall in love with Haiti. The people are very warm. She's read all about the country. The customs. The food. Which is French Creole in origin. I'd like to buy a hand-carved drum with authentic voodoo symbols painted up and down the sides. And a stretched goatskin tambourine that I can use when I'm back home to teach Israeli folk dancing to the neighborhood on Lynn Avenue.

I'm still not sure *why* Haiti. After Miami Beach, Jerusalem is my parents' first choice. Until we're booked on the *Queen Victoria*, I never, ever hear Marvin discuss that part of the world. At the Felman dinner table.

But I am wrong. There's a lot I don't know about Marvin, who is actually interested in everything. Including the French West Indies. For instance, Christopher Columbus, who may or may not have been a Jew, landed on Haiti during his first voyage in 1492. The reason we're going to Port-au-Prince specifically is not because it's the capital but because it's where the Jews lived. And Marvin has an insatiable curiosity about anyplace where Jews live. Or have lived. (Although he'd prefer to read the true-life account at home. Rather than visit the anthropological, socially significant site in person. That's the difference between Edith and Marvin. She's an in-person kind of gal.)

I am nervous about this cruise. Traveling together as a single unit. Edith feels strongly about all of us being together. Our quarters are very close. On purpose. My mother dreams this arrangement into existence. There's no escape. Edith brings her *Shabbos* candlesticks along to light in the King's Dining Room on Friday night right below the shimmering chandelier. I imagine my mother-the-teacher teaching the entire population—crew and passengers, Jews and Gentiles alike—the Hebrew blessings. Marvin stands to lead the dining room in the *kiddish*, the blessing over the wine. They are a strong winning team. For over forty years. Wherever they go, my parents look for Jews. Or any available, open-minded gentiles who are truly interested in the process of cross-cultural fertilization.

I don't know how I'm going to last sleeping in the

same room with Judy and Jan for ten days. And sharing one exceptionally small bathroom that Judy is in all the time. Brushing her long, brown hair and tweezing her eyebrows into thin arches. Throwing up. I can tell she's throwing up by how many times in a row she flushes the toilet. On the *Queen Victoria* you're only supposed to flush when it's necessary. Essential. That's what it says printed on a small white file card. Framed in black above the toilet. *Keep the Atlantic Beautiful*. Although Judy is very thin we don't know that she suffers, not for another five years, from acute anorexia nervosa. Jan and I have to knock on the bathroom door if we want in. It's quiet in our cabin because my sisters still aren't speaking to me. I wander around the *Queen Victoria*.

I miss the Fontainebleau. The gilded side-by-side mirrors that I wave to in the lobby. Bingo at night. All the sand. In between my toes. Group shuffleboard. Daily Ping-Pong tournaments. Fresh grouper steamed in lime juice, ginger, and scallions. It's a Floridian fish, native to the murky green coastal waters that Edith introduces us to. At the welcome party, the captain of the *Q.V.* greets us with a firm salute. He announces over a booming loudspeaker—heard on all seven decks—that we arrive at Haiti in three days. Actually we don't arrive. At all. We drop a huge steel anchor into the middle of the Atlantic. And climb into the lifeboats. One at a time. That are lowered down. Slowly into the deep, cold water. Slowly. So no one loses her balance. Or falls in. Everybody on the cruise is assigned a seat. After we have our puffy orange life jackets secured around our ever-widening waists, we are rowed into the capital city. I'm just not looking forward to the row in. I feel like I lack anticipation. Edith never does. Lack for anything. In her entire personality.

Dinner is two hours away. Everyone's dispersed throughout the ship. The fun has finally begun. Except I don't know why Judy and Jan aren't speaking to me. This has been going on for three weeks. Edith says just to smile and not take it personally. But it's hard. Usually, at least one of my sisters is speaking to me. It's highly unusual for Judy and Jan to be on the same side. Of anything. On the second deck of the *Queen Victoria* I find the Bridge Room. I'm sure Edith and Marvin are inside. Already. Playing with another Jewish couple.

Edith's arranged a tournament. (Like she always does. At home. Or on vacation.) At the same time every day until we dock. Drop anchor. Right outside Port-au-Prince. There's nothing for me to do. But open the door. And wave. To all the bridge players. Edith and Marvin are sitting in the right-hand corner of the room. Judy and Jan are there too, on the left side. I close the door. Nobody in the Bridge Room really wants to go to Haiti. (Except Edith.) They're happy. Sitting around the card table. Eating Planters dry roasted peanuts.

I go upstairs. Sit on the top deck and read Elie Wiesel. The true story of his life in a concentration camp. How he survived Auschwitz. I bring four of his books with me. *Night, Dawn, Fog,* and *Souls on Fire*. Edith says always bring a book. To amuse yourself. And not be completely dependent on another human being for entertainment. Or help. The thing that impresses me the most is that there is never enough food. Just bread and water. And still they survive. Sometimes the bread is too stale to eat. They have to dip it into cold black coffee. Plus, the food in the camps isn't kosher. The Germans know exactly how to torment the Jews. Mix their milk and meat. Together. Throw in some pork at the bottom of the aluminum soup pot. The sun is shining. Out over the Atlantic. The Nazi soup makes everyone gag.

(What would Marvin have done?) Elie Wiesel is an Orthodox Jew. Like Edith, he's a believer. His faith is strong. And like Marvin in the navy, Wiesel keeps kosher the entire time he is in Auschwitz. That's why he's so thin and emaciated when the camps are liberated. It takes a long time for Wiesel to get his full appetite back. *But would the rabbis have said to eat the soup? With the thick, juicy piece of pork lurking in the bottom of the big pot?* When it's a question of life and death, the Talmud commands us to choose life. Under all circumstances. *Life.* I like reading. About the concentration camps. And cruising. At the same time. The smooth rhythm of the *Q.V.* gliding on the water is a great comfort. I close my eyes.

Edith does not believe in physician-assisted suicide. I do. Years from now I watch my mother suffer. Later, I tell my new girlfriend, Lauren. To pull the plug. On me.

No matter what. Unlike my mother Edith, hope does not flow abundant or spring eternal from my heart. The *Queen Victoria* is a calm, soothing sail. I'm not sick to my stomach. I'm half-way through *Fog*. It's a little depressing. I'd like to talk to someone. About what I'm reading. My feelings. Edith says if my stomach starts to feel queasy. To look straight out at the stunning horizon. Think only happy thoughts. Breathe. In. Out. Slowly. On all family vacations, Edith is in charge. She snaps lots of Kodak pictures. And makes individual scrapbooks with navy blue covers for everyone. She gives them to us on the way home. Before the vacation's even over. "Party" favors.

The Jews never settle comfortably in Haiti. Marvin's lecturing at dinner. Edith's smiling. I don't know how he knows all these facts. But he keeps going. She keeps smiling. While the waiters, all four assigned to our table, quickly take away. Large bowls of onion consommé in clear vegetable broth. Without disturbing the Haitian lecture. Or making any noise. Green chopped parsley bits swim to the surface of the steaming consommé. The other people assigned to our table—the Greenbergs from North Carolina, the Schreibers from Westchester County, and Harold and Elaine Levine from Brooklyn—listen attentively to Marvin, who does a good job public speaking. My father is happy when he has an appreciative audience. His entire face brightens with hope. He loves to feel connected to his people Israel and to fill us in on whatever we don't know. All the missing facts. By the time the heavy steel anchor is thrown overboard in the middle of the cold Atlantic. I know more about Haiti and her beautiful people than I ever know about the modern State of Israel.

On the cruise I do not sleep. I listen to the water lapping right outside the cabin window. I lie awake in the top bunk. Wondering what I did wrong. And thinking about how I can get my sisters to talk to me. Dinner is the worst. I don't say a word. For the entire duration of the six-course meal. No one seems to notice. The Felman unit is having too much fun. Maybe when we get to Haiti. Judy and Jan will be so excited over visiting a foreign country, they'll start talking to me. Hopefully. In the midst of their excitement they will actually forget they aren't speaking to me. And like Edith, they'll want to share their enthusiasm with other family members.

Edith says all you do on a cruise is eat. That's what so special about cruising. One glorious sit-down meal after another. Family affairs. All day long. Inside. Outside. Under brightly painted umbrellas. By the pool. At the counter in the exercise room. In the swivel chairs of the ship's beauty parlor. Which is called Eve's Garden of Earthly Delights. The customers are served finger sandwiches and petites fours. We eat in various dining rooms spread out. Over seven decks. Big, beautiful buffets with ice sculptures of naked men and women holding grapes over their private parts, winged horses, deer, and oversized fruit cups—pineapple and apples glistening in the hot August sun. She's right. That's why people cruise. Nobody ever goes hungry. And we don't.

On the American Plan our eating habits are completely regulated. In addition to three meals a day. There is: a midmorning, midafternoon, midevening, and midnight candlelight snack. And if at any time a single guest on the *Q.V.* is hungry in between regular serving hours, all she has to do is go down to the galley and look for the maître d', who's busy going over the evening menu. Just tell him that you're still hungry. Not completely full. You didn't get enough. He'll take care of it. Anything you want to eat. Immediately. Hot or cold. This is a wonderful thing.

We stand on the top deck, getting our instructions for visiting Haiti. At the last minute Judy decides to stay behind. (She always does.) To have the bathroom to herself. Edith isn't pleased. We come all the way to the French West Indies. So we can be together. But Judy insists. She's not feeling well. Her stomach is bothering her from all the wonderful rich food, which I do not see her eat. But Edith believes her oldest daughter. Illness is legitimate. Excused. Judy stays behind. With her sunglasses on, she waves good-bye as the rest of us climb into the lifeboat. And wait to be lowered down. Rowed smoothly into Port-au-Prince. The Captain's parting words are *Do not drink any water, whatsoever, while visiting.* Beautiful Haiti.

And he advises against eating anything. While we're off the ship. *Cooked or uncooked. Fresh. Raw vegeta-*

bles or fruit. No papayas. Bananas. Or coconuts. Abso-lutely no red meat. Not a single chicken breast or grilled barbecue wing. No nuts. Almonds or pistachios. Do not be tempted to taste anything. No matter how good it looks. Or smells. Enticing to the senses. A glorious dinner awaits us in the King's Dining Room. Upon our return. From our exhausting, exhilarating sight-seeing day. The captain promises. An extra special feast. Imitation Haitian style. Since we are advised to look at the real thing. But not taste it. For our own gastronomical safety. The crew knows we'll be hungry. Starving. Seeing the sights always gives the passengers on the *Queen Victoria* an appetite.

I eat a huge breakfast. Before being lowered into the Atlantic with Edith who's snapping Kodaks, Marvin who's talking Israeli politics to his brand-new best friend, Harold Levine, and my middle sister, Jan. Who is still not speaking to me. One more time the captain warns against eating or drinking because it's not clean. At the last minute he adds the very important caveat: *Be careful where you walk. And sit. Recently there is some mild agitation building up. Against the lack of government services. For the Haitian people.*

From the cold waters of the Atlantic I hear the beat of a drum. Then two. And three. Louder and louder. It looks like the entire population of Port-au-Prince— mothers, fathers, children, aunts, uncles, cousins—is at the dock waiting to greet us. Laughing. Smiling. Waving. I have never seen anything like it. Such a welcome for the Jews. This is the warmth Edith talks about. That she reads in all the brochures. Everyone is dancing. Clapping their hands. The women circle the men. As we get closer to shore, I study the steps. To see if there is any resemblance between the Haitian foot-work and the hora, an Israeli circle dance done at cele-brations: Bar Mitzvahs, weddings, anniversaries.

We are rowed right into Haiti. The whole lifeboat is excited. Eager for adventure. We've been out on the high seas for three days. We can hardly wait to set foot on dry land. Marvin jumps up on the dock. To help the crew bring the lifeboat in. And then he shakes hands with the first Haitian to approach him. As soon as we land, we are surrounded by people who ask us for help. Food. Tennis shoes. Socks. Toothpaste. Toilet paper from the *Q.V.* Soap. Peanuts. Bottled water. Coca Cola. Bread. Camel filter cigarettes. We bring nothing with us. As instructed. We leave all valuables behind. The Haitians offer to pose for photographs. In exchange for money. American dollar bills. Singles.

For the first time since leaving the Port Authority. Nothing looks like Edith's brochures. My mother is dis-appointed. She's not saying anything. Upside down cardboard boxes are everywhere. Up and down the dirt road. On both sides. I peek inside. One big box. Is full of sleeping children. Piled one on top of the other. And smaller than our exceptionally small bathroom on the *Q.V.* I keep walking. Ahead. Don't look back. A skinny dog jumps at my heels. I am afraid of dogs. So is Edith.

The dust is in my eyes. Even Marvin is quiet. The entire time we walk the streets and dirt paths of Port-au-Prince, we are approached by hungry, starving people who have that weary, piercing look in their eyes.

This is not a vacation. Staring at hungry people. One cardboard box says U-Haul in block letters. A single electric light bulb hangs off a wire. The bulb is on. How electricity works in a U-Haul box, I don't know. I can't stop staring. What happens to the cardboard box when it rains? I want to run back to the dock. Jump on board the lifeboat. Go back to my top bunk where I lie awake at night thinking about why Judy and Jan don't speak to me. What I did wrong. After an hour Marvin decides it's much too hot to tour. I know. He's acutely uncomfortable. But he won't say. He doesn't want to see the casinos. Or Baby Doc's palace. He doesn't gamble or drink rum. (Which is why people come to Haiti.) Under his breath he says. Never. Coming back. To Haiti.

We should have known. Haiti isn't for the Felmans. Jews are never able to settle comfortably on the land. Marvin explains. In the late 1700s the French don't permit us to build a synagogue. A school. Or a *mikva*. For our ritual baths. We have to import the rabbi. The cantor. And the kosher butcher. Eventually the French expel all the Jews from Haiti. Even after the famous slave revolt, which Marvin reads about, wanting to know more, the Jews can't make a home for themselves in Haiti. We never integrate successfully. Become an essential part of the culture like we do in America. G-d Bless America.

After the French are forced to leave, the Haitians don't trust us. Marvin says we are the middlemen again and again. Wedged in tight. Between the master and the slave. The French use us to run their sugar plantations. The People of the Book can read and write. The Jews want to belong. Wherever we are. No one has a good time. In Haiti. Everyone prefers cruising the Atlantic. Safely on board the *Q.V.* We never go back. I know why we go to Haiti. Because Edith wants to see the world. And Marvin is proud that he can afford to take his whole family on a cruise. Even if it is August, off-season rates. And too hot to travel. Next time. We should know better than to try someplace new.

The last night on board. There is a talent show. We have all become one big, happy family. Crew and passenger. Jew and gentile. Young and old. Except Judy. Who refuses to get dressed up. She stays in the cabin. Jan goes as a *Queen Victoria* cheerleader. In the Arts and Crafts Room she makes her own blue-and-white crepe paper pom-poms. She wears a blue velvet miniskirt and a white turtleneck. With a big "V" sewn in the middle. Right below her budding breasts. On her size six feet. She wears tennis shoes. That she refuses to give away. And one-hundred-percent cotton bobby socks.

Edith and Marvin dress collectively. As a Grimm brothers' fairy tale. Marvin dresses up like Little Red

Riding Hood. Complete with red cape, a hood that Edith makes from her *Q.V.* beach towel, and a bread basket (borrowed from the King's Dining Room) filled with leftover croissants. Marvin wraps another towel around his waist. A skirt. He has great legs. Edith is the wolf. She puts a paper bag over her head and cuts out two ears that stand straight up. Alert. To her surroundings. The wolf has a long tail that Edith makes by tying one pillowcase to another. And another. She pins the finished tail to her behind. It's a long tail that she whips around the cabin. When she walks.

I turn myself into a palm tree. Head to toe. I wrap brown crepe paper around my entire torso. From a string around my neck I hang huge palm leaves that I cut out of cardboard and paint green. Stuffing small brown paper bags with toilet paper and stapling them shut, I make coconuts. That I string together and hang underneath the palm leaves. Little Red Riding Hood carries me down three flights of stairs to the grand ballroom. I cannot walk because my legs are bound. I stand erect. My palm leaves flapping in the air conditioning. The Master of Ceremonies walks over to me. It's too arduous. I can't hop all the way to the center of the floor. Where the strobe lights are shining. He inquires about the nature of my identity. I tell him I am a palm tree. Blowing in the cool tropical breeze. That Haiti made a big impression on me. The applause is very loud. Thunderous. For me. I win first prize: an individual set of hand-painted india ink and watercolor menus of all the meals we eat on board. Authentic Haitian scenes painted on every page. Edith is pleased with the descriptions of the food and the drawings of the country that we visit for an hour.

When we arrive at the Port Authority. Judy and Jan are still not speaking to me. Aunt Shirley and Uncle Nathen greet us at the dock. *How was the trip?* Everyone talks at once. The food is terrific on the *Queen Victoria*. Three full meals a day. The American Plan is a real bargain. Candlelight snacks at midnight. The ice sculptures are magnificent. They never melt. No one mentions Haiti. Ever. It's like we never leave the ship. The whole seven days. I do not dream up our Haitian excursion. I buy a drum. With the sacred spirit of voodoo carved up and down the sides. I beat out a mystical rhythm.

Next August. We return to our connecting end rooms at the Fontainebleau. On the high floor. The maître d' is pleased we're back. He misses us. Marvin's apple blintzes are on the way. Bingo is bigger and better than ever. No matter how much Edith wants to see the world—new exotic faraway places. And break out of our primary, identifying sociocultural category. We always end up right back where we started. Miami Beach. Off-season. There's no place like home.

Lunch in Seattle

EVERY FALL my mother flips every mattress over. It gets the lumps out and they last longer. Sometimes I help her.

Upstairs, under my oldest sister's orthopedic Sealy mattress, my mother finds stored away an entire candy store. No one in the family has any idea how long the candy has been there and why there aren't any baby ants crawling around, in between the blue flannel sheets and the one-hundred-percent cotton blankets. Everything is arranged neatly in rows and in alphabetical order. Judy hasn't taken a bite out of a single candy bar or opened any of the extra-large movie-size boxes of M&M's. She is merely stockpiling. "Hoarder!" my mother whispers in horror into the bedroom. My sister Judith Elaine Felman, oldest of three girls whose names all begin with the letter "J," is a Jewish female hoarder.

I make a list. That I save forever without knowing why.

Granny Smith caramel apples wrapped in gold foil, pink bubblegum, which we aren't allowed to chew, five boxes of Jujube Fruits, three boxes of Good & Plenty, two big bags of M&M's—peanut, one box of peanut brittle, a whole nine-by-eleven-inch aluminum tray filled with walnut peanut butter fudge. A single package of Reese's peanut butter cups, including a dozen Mr. Goodbars, my father's favorite. He loves nuts. And one hundred miniature Snickers—bite size. Ten bags of red and black shoestring licorice, five multicolored popcorn balls wrapped in red cellophane, and Fannie Farmer birds' eggs—white speckled candy-coated malted milk balls sitting in their own nest of mint chocolate twigs that the mattress totally squashed.

It is a beautiful scene, all that candy lined up under my oldest sister's Sealy mattress. She is very neat. I am twelve years old. Judy is a sophomore in high school and a Scotchette, which means she kicks her right leg into the air while at the same time dancing in a straight line in a red and green plaid Scottish kilt and a matching little pillbox hat at all the football games, even on *Shabbos*. Which my father doesn't like, but he agrees to the concession because, after all, we're not in Russia anymore. This is America. My mother cries for days after finding everything hidden away. I don't know why she is so upset. It's not the worst thing that could ever happen—like being hit by a hit-and-run driver the po-

lice never find and then there's a problem with the insurance. After she discovers the candy my mother has
the whole room professionally cleaned and disinfected
with lemon-scented ammonia because she hates ants.
No one ever mentions the sweet stash under the mattress again. Instead, for the next three months we talk
about how the room smells like the scent of fresh-
squeezed lemons mixed with ammonia. It's like it never
happened. Only I never forget. My mother throws
everything away. Immediately.

Then we flip the mattress over.

I want to ask my sister what she was doing with all
that candy and where she bought the Granny Smith
caramel apples, because they weren't in season. And
why weren't the apples rolled in chopped pecans; they
taste better that way. There are so many things I want
to ask Judy.

Like when is the first time and why did you start
stealing in the first place? This I never understand. I'm
too afraid of getting caught. (Although, recently I
started stealing myself—just a single white terrycloth
robe from the Club Level of the Sheraton Commander
on Garden Street in Cambridge, Massachusetts, which
I plan to give back as soon as I order an identical one
from Victoria's Secret.) Weren't you afraid? I'm afraid.
The doorbell is ringing. Nonstop. My mother hates the
noise. She's listening to the Cincinnati Symphony play
Aaron Copland's *Appalachian Spring,* guest conducted

by Leonard Bernstein; they're at the wide open prairie part where the sun's just coming up and stretching out over the horizon of the new frontier. I know my mother's happy. The conductor and the composer are both Jews. (And *feygelahs*, Yiddish for little flighty birds.) And proud of it. Leonard Bernstein never conducts on the High Holidays. Closing her eyes occasionally and humming along as Copland's new day dawns, she prepares dinner: breaded kosher veal chops that always leave grease spots on the ceiling because my mother doesn't have a cooking fan, chunky Mott's applesauce, and baked Idaho potatoes with Fleischmann's pareve butter—nondairy yellow spread—when the doorbell rings nonstop. She tells me to get it. But I don't want to. I have a bad feeling. The front doorbell never rings unless my father is sending my mother flowers for *yontif*. Or there's trouble. Bad news, like when Edith Anne Schear's hair caught on blazing fire wrapped around the defective pink for female G.E. blow dryer. From across the street her mother Betty comes running over crying. Hysterically. (I have to call her Aunt Betty. Which I resent and think is very phony. After all, she's not my biological aunt. And never will be.) We live on a dead-end street. So there's not a lot of traffic when Betty Schear runs over to our side without first turning her head to check for cars in both directions. Edith Anne has long and beautiful golden brown hair that never grows back exactly the same. Betty—Aunt Betty—buys her a lot of hats.

I open the door without looking out the window first. Two men are standing there. Just standing. Staring straight at the *mezuzah*. They've probably never seen one. "It blesses the house," I say. "All Jews have them. We reach up with our fingertips to kiss it, before crossing over the threshold. But you don't have to." The men just stand there. They both have identical brown fedora hats on their heads. They are the exact same height. For a minute I think they are fraternal twins— my father's long-lost relatives from the Holocaust who looked us up in the phone book. We're easy to find. We're the only Felman without a "D," which I always tell people is floating around in the Long Island Sound. Near Ellis Island. We lost the "D." I don't want to let the men in. Because I know that my life will never be the same again. So I stall. I don't want things in the family to change. Ever. We stand staring at each other through the screen for at least five minutes. I smell the veal chops frying. My Dad will be home any minute. I don't know what to do. I am twelve years old. My Bat Mitzvah is six months away. The problem is, when I open the door nothing is ever the same again. I have to practice my Hebrew. Now. *Baruch Atah Adonai . . .*

The men sit in the living room waiting for my father to come home from work. My mother decides to bake the Idaho potatoes while we're all waiting together in the living room. *Elohainu Melach Ha Olam . . .* My middle sister, Jan Ellen, is there too. So is Judy Elaine, who is not saying a word. I don't know why they made my middle name start with an "L" for Lynn, just like the street we live on, because it doesn't go with my sisters' middle names, which both begin with the letter "E." I hear my father drive up the driveway. He doesn't have a real first name, just an initial. "H." His mother didn't want him to be called Hank. He doesn't need a key; I already unlocked the back door. "Smells good." That's the first thing he says. He's talking about the breaded kosher veal chops, not the scent of fresh-squeezed lemons. Everyone in my family has an excellent sense of smell. We got it from my mother, Edith Jeanne. She's French. Then my father, H. Marvin, walks into the living room and looks around. No one says a word. The men get up and introduce themselves. And that's when my life changes and is never the same again. Ever. The family starts to fall apart right there in the living room when the two men get up and walk slowly toward my father. I feel the exact moment when it happens, when the family starts to cave in. I never forget. The look on my father's face. It was the look on my father's face. Exactly six months before my Bat Mitzvah. *Asher Kidshanu B'Mitzvah Tov . . . Holy One of Blessing, Your Presence fills Creation . . . Making us holy with Your Commandments . . .*

The men are undercover police agents who have come to arrest my sister Judy. No one moves. Or says a thing. I keep practicing my Hebrew. Silently, in my head. Judy has been stealing clothes. For months: designer skirts, silk blouses, mohair sweaters, black velour

pants. For months. The two men have had her under
surveillance and they have it all on film. They want to
know what she's done with all the merchandise. For
weeks. They followed her from store to store. Elder
Berman's, Rike's, the Metropolitan, and Donoff's. Then
back to Elder Berman's for a pair of black tights to
match the black velvet skirt from Donoff's. All the
stores want to press charges. I imagine the men in their
matching brown hats following my sister Judy all
around downtown Dayton. She carried a large Samsonite suitcase, they said. Awfully big suitcase for a little
girl. Packed everything away like she was going on a
trip. And never coming back. Home. I never liked
downtown Dayton. It's all very flat; and there's nothing
there. Except National Cash Register, Firestone Tires,
and Wright Patterson Air Force Base a little past downtown. Even the Bosnia peace talks can't save Dayton or
any of its inhabitants. All the international negotiators
do is complain about the food. And ask where the golf
course is.

None of us knows that she is being followed. The entire time. What did my sister do with all the designer
clothes? How did she get them into the house, through
the kitchen, and upstairs without anybody noticing?
We follow Judy upstairs into her bedroom. (I know the
clothes aren't under the mattress because that's where
she stored the candy.) I can't imagine where she put
everything the men say she stole. She opens her closet
without speaking and pushes all the clothes to the left,

clearing the stairs to the attic. We walk up the stairs in single file, the way the Scotchettes march out onto the football field before getting into formation to spell "Go Team" or "Win." In the attic, just like under her mattress, she has lined everything up. My sister is very neat. The rows are perfectly straight. There's a gorgeous Liz Claiborne sweater on the top, third pile, navy blue, that I want to ask if I can borrow before she has to give it back to the store. It's a mock turtle-neck. My mother gasps. Jan and I just keep staring. The men take out notebooks from their pockets and start checking things off. My father doesn't say a word. He has that look on his face. How did we get this far along without someone noticing something? I don't understand. What will happen to my sister Judy. To me. To the whole family. We disintegrate slowly, very slowly, hardly noticeable at first. In fact, I don't really notice until I am forty years old and my mother is already dead and gone that the Felmans fell apart. Utterly and completely. Then suddenly, I can't remember any of the Hebrew I'm supposed to memorize. For my Bat Mitzvah.

My sister is a *gonif*. A real, true-life Jewish princess thief. At twelve, I know without being told that I must never tell anyone about my sister Judy. I swallow hard. This is only the beginning. She steals. For years. Even from us, her very own *mishpachah*. We can't make her stop. I don't understand. Why is she doing it? To me. To my precious mother and father. Only we never, ever talk about it. First there is the candy hidden under the mattress; then there are the clothes. After that, there are the priceless art books from Emerson College: Picasso, Braque, Matisse, van Gogh, and Miró, which come years later when my mother finds them in the basement, in an old footlocker Judy has sent to Dayton from Boston. She insures the trunk for over ten thousand dollars. No one ever knows why. Until my mother opens the trunk when she is searching for old family photographs. Inside each book, stamped in small black block letters, is: *Property of Emerson College. Do Not Remove from Premises under Penalty of Law.* Edith sits down and cries on the hard, cold floor. Then goes upstairs and immediately writes Emerson College an apology note without signing her last name. She never tells my father what she finds. Quietly, she enlists my help. We wrap each book in white tissue paper, pack them in Jaffa orange boxes from Israel, and send them back to Boston anonymously—but insured—only ten years after they were surreptitiously removed from the premises. They're in excellent condition. My mother doesn't say a word when I gently but quickly slip the Brancusi sculpture book out from under the pile and add it to my own personal art book collection. Brancusi is my favorite, not *The Kiss*, but the more abstract *Bird in Space*.

But at this moment I watch my mother watch her husband, who parks cars for a living, beg with all his might the brown-hatted gentile men not to arrest my oldest sister, Judy. *Yehudit* in Hebrew, which means

"Jewess" or female Jew. Judy never liked her Hebrew name. The first American-born Felman grandchild. She can't go to jail. She has to go to college. He'll take care of it, he promises the *goyim*. It will never happen again. He will see to it personally. He is almost crying. His father from Russia is still alive. They park cars together on the lot they finally bought. After working seven days a week, including *Shabbos*. Like small shop-keepers, father and son, except they are parking lot attendants. They wear carmel-colored uniforms with red name tags. So the gentiles aren't afraid. And my grandmother Eva—a beautiful name derived from the Garden of Eden—takes the tickets. Eva—Nanny—speaks English. And knows all the regulars. I always wave when my mother and I go shopping and pull into the parking lot. It will be horrible. If word ever gets out about Marvin's daughter. This is what they came to America for, my grandparents. No one ever says a word. The silence is like children's red Robitussin cough syrup; it suppresses all the congestion in my throat until I am completely quiet and can sleep through the night. All those years. I sleep through the night. Only I don't know it. Couldn't have guessed that I really was taking notes, writing it all down, storing every memory inside, holding the images forever, until the day I would write it all down. And swallow. Before I choke. And swallow.

The trouble with Judy is there from the start. And it never goes away. This is the truth. Only no one wants to admit it. So I have to write it all down. I am just trying to make sense of what happened in my nuclear family. To cause the explosion. The only thing my parents ever fight over is matzo balls. Marvin likes his hard. So hard they barely stay afloat in the warm golden broth that simmers on the stove for hours until the orange carrots, white pearl onions, and green parsley all dissolve. Edith likes hers soft. Fluffy. Floatable. There is no middle ground. My sister Judy is the firstborn. One year after the State of Israel won her independence from the G-ddamn British, Judy was born, caught in between the matzo balls, Edith and Marvin, and the infamous White Paper. The Russians and the French. Jews. They were all Jews, but who could tell from the matzo balls. Judy was the messianic hope after the Holocaust, although no one ever said so directly. It was a lot of pressure. I don't think the trouble was Judy's fault. No one knew what to do. When she was born. She was the first. Of everything. When Israel was born everybody knew what to do: Plant trees. Make the desert bloom. Grow Jaffa oranges, export them all around the world, and plant more olive trees. When all the Jews died in Germany we said *Kaddish*. And never stopped. Saying *Kaddish* for our lost dead relatives and lighting *Yahrzeit* candles for the rest of our entire lives. When Judy was born, it just wasn't her fault. No one knew what to do. She wasn't a boy. There was no *brit milah* or circumcision. This was long before female naming ceremonies became popular. But the problem is, a name and a foreskin aren't even close.

So with Judy it was different. From the beginning. After stealing there was starving. Herself. Nobody noticed at first. All the Felman girls were always trying to lose weight. But it was hard. Because we were hungry. All the time. And we were supposed to eat. Everything. A Jew should never go hungry again. (We were the post-Holocaust generation and future kibbutzniks. The Nation of Israel lives.) My mother had to hide the Chips Ahoy cookies and the Esther Price candy or there wouldn't be any left for my father. We always found the Esther Price candy. Opened the box and ate the milk chocolate caramel pieces from the second layer. No one likes dark chocolate in my whole family. Judy taught Jan and me how to put the lid back on the box and wrap the red ribbon around the gold foil to make the box appear undisturbed. She was our big, older sister. Desperate, my mother finally hid Esther Price in the basement freezer. There is an atomic bomb shelter built into our basement on Lynn Avenue. My mother stores the Passover dishes in the bunkers. "It's the best place for them," she says. "They won't break." On Saturday nights, as soon as our parents go out, Judy leads us down the stairs to the freezer. We stand behind her in line as she hands us all the Empire kosher chickens, one after another. An entire month's supply of poultry. There in the back, stacked neatly in rows, are boxes and boxes of Esther Price. It takes us at least four weeks to go through every box eating just the bottom layer of chocolate caramels. We sit down on the hard, cold cement floor in the middle of the bomb shelter, which is very small and doesn't have a single window. There isn't much air. They're hard to chew frozen. There isn't even time for the caramel to defrost. So we suck fast, melting the milk chocolate on our tongues. We never get caught. No one says a word. That was when all Judy ate was candy.

Or baby shrimp cocktails whenever we ate out at restaurants because that was the only time we were permitted to eat *treif*, nonkosher food. We had a lot of rules to follow. Except for Marvin, who made all the rules up himself and who his whole life kept kosher. Even in the navy. My grandmother Eva from Russia sent him jars of Peter Pan chunky peanut butter, Hebrew National salamis, thick, dark rye bread, and Smucker's seedless strawberry preserves. The whole family was so busy with Marvin's rules, no one noticed that Judy was starving. Herself.

All through high school. There was just too much going on. With Israel, the Suez Canal, the Seven Day War, and the parking lots. Martin's letter from Birmingham and Malcolm's conversion; Bull Conner and the water hoses. Barking German shepherds, Vietnam and the fall of Saigon on TV every night at dinner. And Barbara Walters—the first woman and Jew(ess) to host the *Today* show, whom my father's father from Russia didn't like because he couldn't understand a word she said. She has a slight lisp. Plus Nixon and Kissinger, a self-loathing German Jew who got married to that really tall, lanky blonde Nancy, a *shiksa*, on *Shabbos* and was an embarrassment to us all. The parking lots needed new yellow stripes so all the gentiles would know where to park. Whenever there was a snowstorm my father got up at 4:00 A.M. to shovel and plow for all his customers. There was just too much going on when my oldest sister Judy was growing up. To almost notice her at all.

When the war wasn't on we were busy watching John F. Kennedy, Jr.'s final salute farewell and Jackie's elegant black fishnet veil covering those huge, sad, brown, grieving eyes. Crying herself, my mother said Mrs. Kennedy had such dignity. Until she went and married that short Greek god. There was also the first polio vaccine, invented by Dr. Jonas Salk, another Jew. We were all very busy going to the high school to stand in a straight line to swallow the miracle drug from little white paper cups. It had a horrible taste. The vaccine. Even if it was going to save my limbs from life in a big heavy wheelchair. The war went on and on. McNamara lied, U.S. tanks got caught in the mud so Johnson couldn't run for a second term. Every night. They counted the bodies. On TV and the radio. There was just too much going on to notice that Judy, my oldest sister, firstborn, had stopped eating. Almost disappeared.

And she couldn't play Chopin no matter how many times Edith made us listen to Horowitz after he left Russia. He suffered from melancholia; my mother wanted us to hear the great sorrow in his music. To give us depth. I understood Vladimir's dilemma: he was homesick. Judy hated classical music and sports, especially softball, which we had to play every Fourth of July and Labor Day. As soon as Marvin's team won, we had to run in from the outfield at the end of our dead-end street to eat grilled hamburgers (well done) and kosher knockwurst on pareve egg and onion yellow sesame buns. With hot mustard from the Second Avenue Deli in New York. Whether we wanted to or not. Taken altogether it was just too much. The only thing for Judy to do was to stop eating. Altogether. This was before anorexia and bulimia were discovered in highly successful, extremely insecure, gender ambivalent adolescent females. This was before the postmodern, existential narrative of middle-class Jewish girls living in the Diaspora outside the State of Israel was understood in terms of a historical complex and backlash against the success of the immigrant/refugee generation. Judy was the first grandchild. And she never recovered. From the huge burden of representation. I'm just beginning to understand that it only got worse.

We are having lunch. I am; Judy watches me. Eat. We are together for the first time in years since the moment when Judy is lost to the entire family for one whole month. We don't know where she is. My father refuses to call the FBI. He loathes governmental interference in his private affairs. I picture her wandering around the face of the earth, cold and hungry, starving, looking for something—anything—familiar. She doesn't write or call. But Marvin says not to worry. Four weeks later my father is able to locate his oldest daughter and firstborn because of a parking ticket. Which she receives for leaving her car longer than the thirty-day maximum period allowed at the airport in Hartford. The officials trace the registration to my father in Dayton. (He flies to Hartford by himself to pick up the car before it is towed away and sold in a police sale. And drives it all twelve hours back to Dayton by himself.) Judy drives to the airport one day when she is visiting me. This is the last time I see her until now. Without saying good-bye. She leaves the car, an old Chevy wagon, at the airport parking lot and hops on the first plane to Seattle. She flies standby. Later, I find a note crumbled up in the dried fruit bin in my refrigerator that's nearly impossible to read. "Thanks J. for everything. I have to get out of here. Love, J." I worry. My oldest sister, who is thirty-three, just ran away. From me.

Judy ends up in Seattle via USAir. We don't know where she got the money for the ticket. It turns out, she buys only a one-way fare. She has no intention of returning. My guess is she's been saving up for this, her great escape from the Felmans. She is living at home—temporarily—in Dayton after her divorce from John, a multilingual French Jew whom she met in Port Hardy, British Columbia. Where she went to teach autistic children how to talk after she graduated from Ohio State with a bachelor's degree in education. Everyone

was surprised she actually finished school and graduated. Jan is the brain in the family. She plays the flute
with her eyes closed so she can concentrate better. Judy
got the looks. I got all the leftovers. It makes my mother
mad whenever I say this. But it's true.

Judy is trying to decide what to do next. After John.
I can't remember his last name. She was the first in the
family to get a divorce. Statistically, at the time, American Jews had a much lower, almost nonexistent divorce
rate compared to the rest of the population. Now we've
caught up and there are no more statistics to keep. Except concerning intermarriage. Jewish survival is at
stake in the Diaspora. No one is prepared for the divorce. We didn't even know Judy got married until her
machatanim, the in-laws, write Edith and Marvin for-
mal letters of introduction explaining who they are and
that they love Judy like a daughter of their own and
hope my parents will do the same with their wonderful
son, John. When we go upstairs, my parents lock Jan
and me in their bedroom and tell us they have something important to say. They hand us each a letter. One
is from Fred, John's father, an orthodox Jew, and the
other is from his mother Ruth, a much more secular ob-
server of the faith; they were born in Germany. And im-
migrated to Israel as soon as they could. But one of the
children was blind so Fred moved the whole family to
Canada. In the '50s in Israel it was too hard to make the
desert bloom and at the same time create services for
the disabled. My mother has a party anyway, after the

wedding that none of us or her friends is invited to. She used to describe the *chupah* that Judy, her firstborn, would stand under on her wedding day. Jews always marry after the sun sets on *Shabbos* or in the late afternoon on Sunday. In her dreams the *chupah* is all fresh flowers, pink-, red-, and salmon-colored alstroemerias braided with white baby's breath with light green ferns woven in and out between the flowers. Instead, my mother orders a crushed almond marzipan cake for the party and has the baker decorate it with miniature tangerine Japanese roses. By the time we find out about Judy's Canadian marriage on the island of Port Hardy, astromarias aren't in season.

After her divorce, Judy is hospitalized because she is so thin. I don't even know how long she is married. Nobody says exactly. Three times a day, on her plate she puts three big macrobiotic pills. This is what she eats. All she eats. She has developed a thyroid condition: this is what they say. She's in Dayton and as soon as she's released from Good Samaritan she decides to visit her sisters. Me first. Marvin thinks this is a good idea; he agrees to pay for the trip because he and Edith need a break. Judy never makes it to Jan, our middle sister in Philadelphia. She just goes right to the airport after seeing me for twenty-four hours. And then I don't hear from her again until we're having lunch—I am—in Seattle. Judy watches. Me eat. Finally, my sister asks the waiter to bring her a single order of baby shrimp cocktail with spiced tomato sauce for dipping and dunking. There are very few calories in shellfish.

She's so thin I can barely look at her. I see her scalp exposed beneath her thin black hair, which used to be thick and luxurious. Now it looks like straw. Her eyebrows are all plucked out and penciled in slightly unevenly. This will make my mother cry because Judy was the first baby born at Good Samaritan Catholic Hospital with a full set of thick, dark eyebrows. Through her skin, I see her veins. Blue. There are crucifixes in the birthing rooms. My oldest sister Judy has become a concentration camp survivor. I don't know what to say. She has a huge, extremely soft leather Gucci shoulder bag that she keeps on her lap and cuddles the whole time we sit at the table. She must be cold. We haven't seen each other for so long—years—I can't even remember the last time. I want to ask her if she's still stealing; how else could she afford a Gucci bag? Judy has expensive tastes. I know I'm not supposed to say anything. Our mother Edith is very sick. She has Parkinson's and shakes when she's rigid and can't move. Judy has always identified with my mother. I don't know why exactly. I can't understand what she's saying. Sitting across from her my vision blurs. I am trying not to cry. This is my biological sister. Flesh of my flesh. We're at the Four Seasons in Seattle; I plan to send the bill to Marvin. This is family. For dessert I order a plate of homemade petits fours. And a decaf cappuccino. Seattle is the cof-

fee capital of the U.S.A. Petits fours are my mother's
favorite: chocolate iced, mocha, butterscotch, and almond. With little dabs of red on top. I order one of each.
When they come, I wrap them all up in my white linen
napkin and then I put the small package of fresh baked
goods in my purse. Judy asks the waiter for a glass of
warm milk. I've never seen my sister drink milk. In fact,
she hates milk and stopped eating dairy in high school.
About the same time she began to eat only candy and
baby shrimp cocktails. Which she merely pushes to the
side and doesn't eat at all. I understand; I've almost lost
my appetite too.

When the milk comes, Judy puts on her sunglasses
because the light bothers her eyes with her contacts
on. Then she opens her soft Gucci leather shoulder bag.
I think she is reaching in for a Kleenex tissue to give
me. To dab my eyes. But she's not. Instead, she takes
out a very small, infant-with-its-eyes-closed miniature
schnauzer and hands it to me across the table. No one
in my family likes animals; my mother says most Jews
are allergic to pets. They need too much attention. "I've
got to feed them," she says. "They were just born. I don't
want them to die. Feel how soft the fur is." She takes
another one out and starts spoon-feeding it warm milk.
Afterwards, she removes the French sourdough rolls
from the bread basket and gently puts the little infant
puppy in the basket, careful to cover him up with the
cloth napkin like a wool blanket. I don't want to know
how many puppies she has in there. I'm surprised

they're still alive. We've been sitting here for more than an hour. "They've been sleeping, almost since they were born. I found them. Last week. When I threw away my newspapers. They were sleeping by the side of the road where the garbage gets picked up. Piled one on top of the other." I don't say a thing. I hope my sister didn't steal these schnauzers. I watch Judy feed her baby dogs at the Four Seasons Hotel in Seattle. Filling up the bread basket one by one, they begin to look like a nuclear family. By the time the waiter comes to clear the table, Judy puts all the puppies—there are four of them—in her lap except the one she gave me, which I'm still holding. I am afraid of dogs. I always have been. I don't know what to do. I hand the dog back across the table, careful not to knock over my water glass or the cut crystal vase of fresh tulips. When all the milk is gone, Judy takes her white linen napkin, wipes their mouths dry, and then gently puts each puppy back into her shoulder bag. I get the bill and we get up to leave. I don't look back, ever. Back at my hotel room, I turn on the TV to watch the evening news. I eat my petits fours. One after another. Lining them up on my bed, I start with mocha followed by butterscotch. I eat slowly; these are big petits fours. I don't want to get sick. I save the chocolate iced for last. My mother's favorite.

It's almost two whole years before the Oslo Agreements and three years before Rabin's assassination. Who could imagine a Jew killing another Jew. Ever. But that's the way chaos descends, from the inside out. Before it spreads quickly, over everything. Bill Clinton is running for president with his wife, Hillary. They want national health care for everyone. Judy doesn't have health insurance. She doesn't have a job. Or a car. She left it at the Hartford airport long-term parking lot and my father never gave it back. She takes cabs everywhere. She has developed a stong aversion to public transportation. I don't know why. The moment when Bill Clinton is elected and Maya Angelou reads her "new day is dawning" poem, I know. And when Arafat is invited to the Rose Garden and Rabin finally decides to shake his hand, I know. Nothing will ever be the same again. Ever. I can tell by the look on Rabin's face when he decides to reach out his hand. The last poet before Maya Angelou to read at a presidential inauguration was James Dickey. Carter was president and he served only one term.

He was a small peanut farmer with big ambitions. Like my father, who was a small parking lot attendant with big ambitions. Only Jimmy couldn't free the hostages and Marvin couldn't free Judy. Peanuts and parking. Small failures—global implications. *Or L'goyim*, a light unto the nations. The Jews are supposed to set an example. Judy was supposed to set an example for Jan and me. Her younger sisters. Only it was too much. She gave the schnauzers away. "I wanted to keep them," she says to me, long distance, months after our lunch in Seattle. "But I just couldn't feed them anymore. They were hungry all the time. It was just too much."

Hyperventilation

E DITH WASHES my whole mouth out with
Ivory soap. A small hotel-size bar that she puts in
her purse when she's in the *women's restroom* at Howard Johnson's. Edith holds my chin firmly in place. I
can't move. Or wiggle. Out of my mother's firm grip.
This hurts me more than it will ever hurt you. Tears
well in her eyes.

The small bar of Ivory soap is in her right hand.
The water faucet is on. Running warm. *Open up.*
She's slightly hysterical. Calmly, I open my mouth. The
calmer I am, the more agitated Edith becomes.

The is the first time Edith washes out my entire
mouth with soap. Which tastes awful. I wonder. Did
her mother do this to her? Growing up in Wheeling,
West Virginia? After she opens her mouth in front
of all the gentiles and says something awful? Ivory
soap is dry. It flakes. Edith is shaking. She sticks the

bar under the warm water. *Don't swallow. Or you'll choke.*

I choke. Once. Twice. I cough. I spit. Edith is frozen with fury.

The house on Lynn Avenue is very quiet. I am twelve years old. I feel very close to Edith. Who is livid. Because I said the "F" word. Out loud. *I didn't know you even knew that disgusting word. I don't want to hear you say it again. Not in this house. Or anywhere else. For that matter. Ever.*

The "F" word just pops. Out. Loudly. (From deep within my passive vocabulary that I normally save for Scrabble tournaments with Marvin.) Without any prompting from me. Like a tease. All I do is open my mouth. And out pops the most red hot, forbidden word. In the Felman household. I don't even know. Exactly. What the word means. Why it's so bad. What the fuss is all about. But clearly. The mere sound of that dirty, filthy word. Is too much for Edith.

I walk past my oldest sister Judy sitting on the steps in the hallway with her football star. Called Bo. As in "bow and arrow." He has blue eyes. Broad shoulders. Is almost six feet tall. And weighs a ton. He's the quarterback at Fairview High School. Judy is in love. But I know. Judy and her blue-eyed quarterback have nothing in common. After graduation she's going to Ohio State University to be a teacher. Like

Edith. He's going to work in his father's hardware store and then join the Army Corps to get an education. I say to the star-crossed young lovers, "What are you two doing? F-U-C-K-I-N-G around?" I laugh at my own joke. In a voice. A little too loud. For my own good.

Edith overhears me. Immediately. She says *Follow me.* I do. Slowly.

We stand near to the sink in the bathroom next to the kitchen. Edith is crying. She's extremely upset. She closes the door. It's just the two of us. Crowded up against the cold sink. I love to be alone with Edith. To have her all to myself. This is a small, half-bathroom. That Edith uses to put her Estée Lauder on in the morning. I watch, sitting on the toilet seat: brown mascara, black eyeliner, hazel green eye shadow, light red glossy lipstick with color coordinated blush. While the coffee is brewing. I don't get it. *What's the big deal.* It's just a word. Not to Edith. Whom I hate to upset. Because most of the time. She and I have a lot of fun together. Now. She won't take me to Howard Johnson's for a mint chocolate chip hot fudge sundae. Until she gets over being mad.

Here. She hands me a glass of cold water. *Rinse.* I rinse my dirty filthy mouth out. In front of my mother. I hate Ivory soap. Both my parents have a thing about the word *fuck* that I don't completely understand. But the older I get and the more of the world past Lynn Avenue I see, the more they hate that dirty, disgusting, filthy word.

And the more I am drawn to it. In all its many forms. Nouns. Verbs. Adverbs. Adjectives. Gerunds.

What the fuck?
She's fucked up.
Stop that fucking noise!

None of which I (or any of the Felman girls) am allowed to say out loud. I learn my lesson. The extremely hard way. From a single bar of dry, cakey Ivory soap. Right before my Bat Mitzvah. When I have to give a speech to the entire congregation of Beth Abraham. That it's not *really* okay to say what you think. Out loud. People, including Edith and Marvin. Just pretend. That they want to know what's on your mind. This is a valuable lesson. For a Jewish lesbian writer to learn. So early in life. And never forget. (That) The whole truth. So help me G-d. Doesn't really matter. (*Who cares if you're Jewish and homosexual. You don't have to tell the whole world. Do you?*)

About a year after I say the forbidden "F" word way too loud and Edith overhears me, I lie down on the locker room floor. I am soaking wet. Right after our basketball game. I'm short for a point guard. But good. Fast. We win the game. I play hard. I score eight points. I'm thirteen. In the eighth grade. I lie down on the cold tile floor. Of Fairview Elementary School. Open my mouth. And close my eyes. Just enough. So it looks like

84

Hyperventilation

I'm really sick. Which I'm not. I feel fine. I breathe. In. Out. Slowly at first. (Like Edith taught me. When I'm not feeling well.) Then faster and faster.

Until I *hyperventilate*. When you hyperventilate. You eventually pass out. I don't know, since I've never hyperventilated before, that soon I shall see stars in front of my eyes and pass out. I've only read about this particular medical condition. In the Healthy Living section of the *Dayton Daily News*. I am wide awake. All the girls bend over me. The whole team. I enjoy the attention. Immensely. The coach calls an ambulance.

For as long as I can remember. I am in love with the *Dr. Kildare* show on TV. I want to be rescued. By his very attentive, black-haired nurse.

And. I long to ride stretched out on a narrow stretcher, strapped in. In the back of a speeding ambulance. With the curtains slightly drawn. So the sun isn't in the dying patient's eyes. The oxygen tank is ready. Just in case. I'm breathing. Harder. Faster. Any minute I will surely pass out. I hear the traffic slow down. The siren wails. It's exciting. I am alone in the back of the ambulance with the medical emergency technicians. A man and a woman. They're talking about me. I don't actually pass out completely. I pretend. I'm an excellent actress. Even at thirteen. I know how to faint. Fall convincingly to the floor of the restaurant whenever we eat out as whole family. Embarrassing everyone. As soon as I stand up. We're seated quickly. At the exact table Edith has her eye on all along. End corner tables are the best. Away from the swinging doors and all the cooking smells in the kitchen. Nowhere near the entrance. Where all the foot traffic. Arrives. And departs.

Generally speaking something is wrong with me. And has been for a long time. Weeks. Months. Years. Only I'm not sure what. Nobody else in the family notices. That anything is wrong. Finally. I wear myself out. Breathing. In. Out. I pass out. The ambulance whizzes by. (Just like I imagined.) With me stretched out in the back. We're almost at the hospital. I don't remember the exact order of events right before I nod off. I wonder how they're going to reach Edith. Her sister, a real-life nurse (Dr. Nurse), Aunt Shirley, is visiting from New York. They're having lunch at Friendly's. Shirley likes the fried clams. Which of course aren't kosher.

Things pick up. When we pull into the Emergency Entrance. The sliding glass doors slide open. The technicians wheel me in. I'm excited. A wee bit nervous. I've dreamed about this moment. For years. Wondering what it would be like to be rushed back to Good Samaritan Hospital—where I am born. And the umbilical cord attaching me to Edith is cut. Forever. I have no idea that when I get up this morning I will not be coming home to sleep in my own bed on Lynn Avenue for a long, long time.

The curtains are drawn all around me. It's noisy. My parents aren't here yet. Neither is Rabbi Schwartz, who is available for private consultation in family emergencies. I am alone. By myself in the hospital. Where people go when they are sick. And ready to die. I quickly understand that I have to keep this heavy breathing up. Or they will send me home. Back to the eighth grade. And out. Into the wide, wide world where I don't want to go. I need a break. That's how this whole thing starts in the first place. Every day. I don't know why. I am so tired.

How to explain the situation to Edith and Marvin, who don't always know exactly what's going on with their three daughters. It's not that they don't care. Because they do. Care a lot. More than any other mother and father on Lynn Avenue. They're wonderful parents. Who work hard. In America. To give their children every opportunity imaginable. Seriously. I ice skate, paint, act, play the piano. And take twirling baton lessons. In a room that has mirrors on all four sides. I watch myself twirl. I join Girl Scouts, participate in the spelling bee every year, try out for cheerleading three years in a row until I am selected to join the squad. And I am an active member of Le Bon Club Français. These are just my secular activities. I also go to Hebrew school, attend religious school, and learn Israeli folk dancing. I belong to Young Judaea, a Zionist youth group. And go to the synagogue with Edith and Marvin every *Shabbos.*

We go on family vacations to Miami Beach. Edith bakes her own delicious thumbprint cookies rolled in chopped pecans with pink and green butter cream ic-

CRAVINGS

ing spooned into the middle of each of Edith's delicate thumbprints. Somehow. It begins to dawn on me. That nothing's working like it's supposed to. A feeling I have developed over time into a wordless ache. Edith and Marvin can't fix everything. Only none of us know this until it's way too late. I want to tell them. Nothing is their fault. Shit happens. But I am not allowed to say that word either. Or think it. Privately to myself.

Things are getting a little out of control. Dr. Kildare's handsome nurse wants to give me a shot in the arm. To calm me down. I hate shots. I thrash all about. Refuse to settle down. Breathe. In. Out. Hard. Fast. I'm getting dizzy. The fluorescent lights are awful. The glare gives me a headache. Just as I am about to pass out. For Real. In. Out. I breathe as hard as I possibly can. The heavy, off-white curtains in my cubicle part.

Edith and Aunt Shirley rush in. From the corner of my eye. I see angels, dressed in white. I have great peripheral vision. They look worried. I never plan to cause this much trouble. To upset anyone. Edith bends down. Close to me. I like to be close to my mother. All alone with her.

Edith puts her hand over my forehead. I calm down. I start to relax. I'm still breathing hard. In. Out. Out of the corner of my eye. Aunt Shirley is holding a brown paper bag. She's whispering to the doctors. Edith's hand moves gently back and forth. Across her baby's forehead. I hope they finished lunch.

I'm petrified. I've been this way for a while. Since

school started six months ago. I'm really scared. Of what. I have absolutely no idea. My parents have big plans. They want all their children to be *happy, attractive, thin, well adjusted. Productive. Contributing. Joyful members of secular society. Then. Marry smart, attractive, successful Jewish men. Join a* shul. *Assume a strong leadership role in the Jewish community. President. Vice President. Chairman of the Social Action Committee. And the Book Review. Have children who get Bar Mitzvahed. Be fruitful, multiply in the years to come. And above all else. Flourish.*

Before I know what's happening. Aunt Shirley, Dr. Nurse, is putting the brown paper Stop & Shop bag over my head. I scream. I kick my small feet into the air. (Edith and I wear the same shoe size.) I can't believe what's happening. Not at all like I imagined. Dr. Kildare's beautiful nurse is supposed to rescue me. Tell me *everything's okay.* I don't have to perform anymore. Edith is letting her sister put a big, brown grocery bag that smells like Clorox detergent over my head. I'm suffocating. I can't make a sound.

Just when I know I'm going to die. Gasp my last breath ever. I hear Aunt Shirley say. *That's it. Enough. It worked. She's calm now. Take the bag away from her mouth.* I am not calm. My own mother stood by and let Dr. Kildare's pretty nurse put a paper bag over my head so I'd settle down and not say nasty little things to all the strangers.

I'm furious. I refuse to speak. This is not like me. I

am normally loquacious. Right now. After five hours of silence. I am wheeled into the elevator. The orderly presses 5. The doors opens. He rolls me into my own room. I am in the children's wing. Where all the kids look pale, yellow, and dying. I'm not sick. Or pale. My face is still flushed. Slightly. From all that heavy breathing.

When the orderly leaves, I am alone again. Edith and Aunt Shirley are filling out the paperwork to admit me. I'm still not talking. To anyone. I begin to remember that I am unhappy. That all my life I have been unhappy. Only no one ever seems to notice. All the Felmans are busy. I never tell them. They don't ask. I don't know what to say. How to explain the situation. Without blaming anyone. Today. After we win the basketball game. I have enough. That's all I remember. I am completely exhausted. I want to sleep in the Good Samaritan Hospital. Maybe even for the rest of my life.

I wake up. Marvin's in the room. Pacing. His baby girl. His Jewish American princess is in the hospital. What will he tell his father, who thinks Marvin spoils his girls. (They argue about this all the time. I don't think any of us are spoiled.) Edith is gone. I hear my father walk back and forth. From the window. To my bed. Someone put the bars up. So I won't fall out. I don't know what time it is. It's dark outside. Marvin's holding a styrofoam cup. And a white plastic spoon. *Here. Your favorite.* My current flavor is Charlie Brownie. Peanut butter swirls. With fudge brownie chunks. Nuts and caramel swishes. All whipped into thick creamy, home-made French vanilla ice cream.

I had them put warm butterscotch sauce on top. And candied red and green cherries. It's nice to see Marvin. Who looks bewildered. Upset. They all come to visit me. One by one. Alone. Never together.

When Jan comes to see me on her thirty-minute lunch break from high school I am surprised. I don't have any idea that she cares. At all. (About me.) *I am worried.* She says. Standing at the foot of my bed. I don't say anything. It's not that I don't want to open my mouth and talk. To my middle sister. I nod. I don't know what to say. Where to start. We cry. Together. Silently.

After Scotchettes and football practice. Judy and Bo walk into my hospital room. Bo—whom Marvin is not happy about—still has his big shoulder pads on. He looks ominous. Judy is dressed in her dancing uniform. A plaid kilt and matching pillbox hat. I close my eyes.

I can never get enough attention. (Judy and Jan feel the same way.) I always feel deprived. There's never enough to go around. I don't know where the hunger comes from. But it's there, inside me, like one giant ache. Since the day I am born. Edith says I cry a lot. The whole first year. Whenever she leaves the room. She can never leave me alone. Judy and Bo hold hands at the foot of my bed. They wave good-bye to me. Edith and I hold hands. When we go shopping.

I don't know what I thought would happen. Re-turning to the hospital. To rest. For a few days. Slowly.

I begin to want my life back. The old way. Before I ever have the bright idea to change the rhythm of my adolescent breathing. I want out. Like Edith. And to be running around. Doing a hundred and one different things all at once. Pushing forward without a single minute to spare. Nothing goes to waste.

Lying in this bed. I realize. It's impossible to go back. To the old way. Nothing will ever be the same again. It's all my fault. Something is set in motion that cannot be stopped the minute I lie down on the cold tile floor. It's time to breathe. Hard. Again. In. Out. Until by accident I press the call button. And the alarm in the nurse's station goes off. In. Out. I don't stop hyperventilating until Dr. Kildare's nurse walks in. And puts her arms around me. Just like Edith always does. When she has time. And is not the president of the PTA or Hadassah. Dorothy in the *Wizard of Oz*. Or knitting seven blue and white cheerleading vests in her free time. And baking seven Lincoln logs for Jyl's third-grade class. Or picking up her parents, Tessie and Al, for *Shabbos*. Every Friday night. Right after she sticks the big, heavy Empire kosher chicken in the oven.

The last person to visit me is Edith, who doesn't stop crying. *You're going to be here for a couple of days.* She shakes her head. She weeps in front of me. Her favorite baby girl. I don't say a thing. This is not at all what I planned to do. When I make my plan. It is to breathe hard. Fast. Gulps of air. Not to stop talking. Although the two seem to work well together.

Everyone is concerned. I have never seen Edith so upset. I wish I could tell her it's not her fault. I bring this on myself. Sleeping in the children's wing. I start to fall asleep while my mother watches over me. When I grow up. I want to be just like Edith. Which is totally impossible. Nobody is just like Edith. But I can try.

They are concerned there is nerve damage. In the brain. I am wheeled upstairs for an EEG. Which means a nurse's aid rubs a lot of petroleum jelly into my hair. So the electric wires with buttons on the end will stick to my head beneath my long, frizzy brown hair that hasn't been washed for days. It's freezing in the laboratory. I need a blanket. The cold temperature is necessary for the efficiency of the test. Edith and Marvin are at work. Judy and Jan are in school. I am in Good Samaritan for over three days. I wonder how to get how awful I am feeling to show up on the brain scanner. I decide to hold my breath. For as long as I can. Create dark spots. Huge ellipsis on the screen.

It doesn't work. Just as I fear. The report comes back negative. *Hello. I'm Doctor Cooper.* He acts like I'm going to answer him. That we are going to have a real conversation. I don't speak to anyone for over three days. Why should I start now? *We need to talk.* This is not the way to get me to open up. I don't think the man is Jewish. If he's not. There's no way I'm going to talk to him. He'd never in a million years understand what the problem is.

My people are in a perpetual state of mourning. We

are hated and loathed throughout the world. Conse-
quently we are filled with feelings of inferiority. And
self-loathing. The Holocaust proved once for all. What
we always know to be true. Is true. This is why the Jews
have to work so hard. To succeed. To be excellent at
everything we do. To set an example. For all the goyim.
This is what Marvin's father says. All the time. On and
on. Over and Over. *In America. We cannot afford a sin-*
gle mistake. Or they'll come after us. Again. And this
time. We won't be so lucky. Technology is more ad-
vanced. Edith and Marvin. Work hard. All their lives.
They take care of their parents. They set an example.
For the entire Midwestern Jewish community. And
their beautiful, talented, brilliant daughters. Who mys-
teriously all have trouble. Fulfilling their own unique
potential. The doctor pulls up a chair. I don't like the
way he smells. He smells.

"Are you Jewish?" I am speaking. I ask that question.
Out loud. I can't believe I opened my mouth. He sits
there. Staring at me for two solid hours. I lie in bed.
Staring at Jesus nailed to the cross. He's up on the wall.
Right in front of me. Good Samaritan is a Catholic hospital. That is open to the general public. But patients
are not allowed to cover up the Lord. Hospital regula-
tions. Like me. Jesus is in perpetual pain. I wonder how
long he stays alive. Before all those nails kill him. The
Son of G-d's flesh. Burns. In total agony. The good doctor smiles. He thinks his method is working.

The Jewish question pops out of my mouth. I did not

plan to ask the man a single thing. Unfortunately. I keep talking.

"If you're not. How do you think you can help me?" *Why.* He wants to know. Is it necessary for him to be a *Jew.* And then he does exactly what I expect him to do. He puts his *goyisha* left foot in his mouth: *Is being Jewish so important to you. That you can only talk to other fellow Israelites?* This is what he asks me. The good doctor and I don't hit it off. From the very beginning. I don't trust the man. I hate him.

He tells Edith and Marvin that their precocious baby is really an enfant terrible in disguise. And that I am incorrigible. Which humiliates me. And brings more shame upon the family. This only compounds the difficult situation. That I get us all into. (Judy and Jan never forgive me. I find out years later. That they are furious at all the attention I get.) I am in the hospital for over a week. Edith is desperate. For a cure. Anything. To fix the situation. Immediately. I want to help her fix things. Fix me.

They want to move you. Edith tries to look at me. But she can't make real eye contact. *To St. Elizabeth's Hospital.* She explains. There's a special ward there. I'll be happier. The service is better. More personal attention. And I'll like the food. Every night, after teaching school, Edith brings me roasted kosher chicken—breasts and wings—covered in layers of aluminum foil to keep the crispy brown bird piping hot. And she defrosts a pineapple noodle kugel that she brings along for all the night nurses. One evening she surprises me. With a whole green pistachio cake. To make me feel better. After she leaves. I eat the entire cake. Bite after delicious green bite. *They're going to move you Monday. In two days.* She walks out of the room. Leaving a plate of warm thumbprint cookies behind that she just took out of the oven. On her way to the hospital. After work.

I am wrecking the family. I can feel it. Nobody has to say a word. My grave illness is supposed to fix things. Make everything better. And make us much closer. As a nuclear family unit: Judy, Jan, Jyl, Marvin, and Edith. Only it's not working. At all like I planned.

Marvin tells me that his cousin Norman and his wife Harriet are going to Miami Beach. There's a linen convention at the Hotel Americana. (Norman is in the linen supply business. He services all the synagogues and Jewish organizations in town. That require fresh, starched, neatly ironed white or light blue linen: All the bar mitzvah and wedding banquets. The guest-of-honor dinners. The Lion of Judaea awards. Where they honor Edith and Marvin. Every couple of years.) Norman and Harriet are leaving Monday for ten days. They'd like to come see me. Before they leave. I'm thinking fast and hard. I don't want any visitors. Except the immediate family.

I know. If I go to St. Elizabeth's. I'll never get out. They will keep me there with Jesus nailed on the cross. Forever. Waiting for a scientific explanation. What's wrong. With me. All I need to get better. Is a little extra attention. From Edith. And Marvin. I want my sisters to like me. So we can be friends. And confide in each other. Which never happens. I need a rest. From trying too hard. To make everyone happy. Rest and relaxation for ten more days. Relief. A little sun. Would do me a world of good. Fresh squeezed orange juice. Swimming in a giant pool. A change of scenery. Shuffleboard. Eating out. At a different delicatessen every day. I decide that Edith and I are going to the linen convention. Only nobody knows but me.

I start to talk on Saturday when Edith comes to visit. Marvin is with his father. I tell her that I'm feeling better. That all I need is a little more rest. Before I go back to the eighth grade. *I'm sorry I scared the whole family. But I'm really much better. Perhaps, instead of going to St. Elizabeth's on Monday. We can go, she and I, with Norman and Harriet to the linen convention. Norman can go to all the meetings. We girls can sit by the pool. Drinking fresh squeezed orange juice. Feeling the warmth of the Floridian sun on our faces. I can get my color back (which is important to Edith.)* I sit up in bed. Smiling.

For the first time in over a week. To show her how much better I feel. Edith smiles back. She wants to believe that what I'm saying is true. That nothing is really wrong with me. That a little fresh Florida orange juice and a good corned beef sandwich sliced extra thin on a fresh bulky onion roll can't fix. Hot mustard. Coleslaw.

Giant dill pickles. None of her girls is ever supposed to be in the hospital. Except to be born and to give birth. To future generations.

When Marvin arrives. Edith is on her way out. I overhear my father and mother talking in the hallway about my plan. Edith says she'll call Harriet. And the Hotel Americana. Edith and I go to Florida. We have a *wonderful* time. Relaxing together. It is the first time since I am born that I have my mother all to myself. No one in the family ever asks me what is wrong the week I hyperventilate. (For over forty years. We never talk about it.) And I don't say. For the next few months. Everything is fine.

Until I hyperventilate at that famous music camp. Where Van Cliburn plays every August. Interlochen. Right outside Grand Rapids, Michigan. Where I am participating in a drama workshop (the Lee Strauss method) for talented, gifted youth. And taking harp lessons, sculpture, sailing, white water rafting. And learning calligraphy with india ink. I'm the cabin representative on the camp council. I'm doing really well. So. I know. It's time to try again. I lie down on the floor of girl's cabin number twelve. My cabin. I hyperventilate. (Just like I did six months earlier.) I don't stop. All the girls in my bunk bend over me. Breathing. In. Out. Hard. Fast. It all comes back to me. I know. Soon. I'll pass out. The counselor calls the ambulance. I am taken away in my favorite position.

I remain in the camp infirmary until Edith flies

USAir across the Midwest. Switching planes in Pittsburgh. To come get me. (She hates to leave Marvin alone.) She wants to take me home. To see a doctor. I tell her. *All I need is a rest*. She wants to believe me. Very much. Edith longs for everything to be okay. She tries so hard. With all her children. To see that we fit into the scene. As her mother, Tessie, did with her. In Wheeling, West Virginia. Blend in. Join the natural flow of events. I keep trying all my life. But it never works. I don't go back to Dayton, Ohio. I go to stay with my mother's only sister. Shirley. In New York. For the rest of the summer. (It's my idea. That way. Everyone will think I'm still acting in plays at Camp Interlochen.) Judy and Jan are furious. I get all the attention. Even though it never feels that way.

For years. Whenever I am afraid. I hyperventilate. Edith flies all over the world. To rescue me. She leaves Marvin alone. Judy and Jan never stop being mad at me. Edith and I never say a word about the whole situation. My entire life. By the time she dies I still don't know what happened in Good Samaritan Hospital when I am in the eighth grade. Marvin is relieved when my life gets back on track. I have much too much to accomplish to be depressed. My whole life. I don't know why. From a very early age. I am always afraid to say exactly what's on my mind.

Everyone can see how well. I'm doing. Growing up in Dayton, Ohio, twirling the baton in a room full of mirrors. From all four sides. I throw the silver baton straight up. High into the air. I turn around. Quickly. I catch the whirling, twirling baton with pastel color streamers in my right hand and bow with my left. I say to myself, looking right at the audience, *Fuck*. It's so easy to please a crowd. All a nice Jewish girl has to do is smile.

White Spots

M ARVIN HAS THE CARPET professionally
cleaned. The spots never come out. Saliva; Folgers mountain-grown decaffeinated black coffee; Diet
Coke; Lipton tea; Tropicana orange juice. Edith's favorite herb tea, Lemon Zinger, leaves a small yellow stain
on the soft, thick, white carpet. From the kitchen to the
dining room, there's a long trail. It's a bad spot. The
bathrooms are carpeted too. The entire apartment,
every room, all the same, all white. Although not the
extremely popular shag style. Edith hates shag. It reminds her too much of living animals. My mother
is afraid. Cats and dogs. Large German shepherds.
Snarling Doberman pinschers. Small black poodles. It
doesn't matter. My father doesn't like dogs.

In the bathroom the spots are antiseptic. Medicinal:
Robitussin red cough syrup, rubbing alcohol, dentist-
recommended Crest toothpaste with Fluoristat, and
wintergreen Listerine mouthwash—free samples from

"Aunt" Betty's husband's office. Pink Oil of Olay facial cream for my mother's sensitive skin. Which changes the texture of the carpet entirely. Because it's oil based. Nonsoluble. There are three kinds of compounds that stain my mother's new white carpet: oil, detergent, and anything alcohol based. Water solubles wash out.

Because of all the spots, I finally begin to see what it is like for my father all the years she is sick and he is home alone. With her. Every day. Trying to hold their life together, keep her comfortable in the wheelchair. And remove the spots before they become permanent stains on the brand new carpet, which she puts down right before they have to leave the house that I grow up in on Lynn Avenue. And move into the Eva Felman Apartments. That Marvin saves all his hard-earned money from the parking lots to build. After a dedication ceremony, like when Jackie Kennedy Onassis lovingly christens Ari's large boat with an exquisite bottle of pink champagne. Marvin names each brick after his mother, my grandmother Eva. Then he hosts a reception in Eva's sparkling new lobby with chocolate and raspberry rugalach, warm—with raisins and nuts—apple strudel, and Folgers mountain-grown decaffeinated black coffee. Poured from a big sterling silver samovar. In Judaism, you can't name anyone or anything after a living person. Not only is it forbidden, it's bad luck and disrespectful. But after they're dead, what is once forbidden becomes a *mitzvah*.

My father's father moves in too, one floor below

Edith and Marvin. It's easier that way. Marvin takes care of both of them. Home health care. At the same time. In the Eva Felman Apartments in downtown Dayton. He prefers it that way. My grandfather isn't sick. There's nothing wrong with him that a quick telephone call upstairs to Marvin can't fix. Except life in America in general. And skyrocketing gasoline prices, which my father's father blames nonstop on the Arab populations of the entire world. Marvin drives his father wherever he wants to go. Which is always food shopping at Kroger's. My grandfather from Russia doesn't like French Jews. They're almost as bad as German Jews. My mother's family is French American. And Jewish. The two families are foreigners to each other. Speaking vastly different languages. In English whole words often mean very different things. Depending on who the speaker is.

Anything yellow is impossible to get out. This upsets Marvin, who likes everything to look good. New. All the time. The worst are the scrambled eggs that my mother's wheelchair rolls permanently into the carpet in the kitchen. On her way out to the dining room. Back and forth. Scrambled yellow is now part of the weave. And the baked mashed potatoes that Marvin buries her L-dopa pills in and then sprinkles with paprika never come out completely. None of the Felmans can stand spots of any kind. All blemishes have to be removed. Immediately. Before they have a chance to sink in. My mother, Edith, is fastidious. Not just about housekeeping, but about everything. Her body. Us—the girls. Marvin. Bathrooms. Closets. Coat pockets. Hair. Front teeth. Her three Js must be immaculately clean. As young Jewish American French Russian girls growing up in America, we learn to put ourselves together with intention and without a single wrinkle ever showing.

That's why it's difficult when Edith gets sick; we don't know until it's too late. For Bayer aspirin. Or even ironing. She has the headaches for years before anyone notices a thing. Or says a word. Jan remembers our mother as depressed. Lying on the couch on Lynn Avenue with her right arm stretched out, covering her forehead. But it isn't depression. It's the headaches. Marvin says his wife is never depressed. She is a happy woman and fun to be with until the moment she gets sick. Edith and Marvin are extremely compatible. Even though my father's family is more religiously observant than my mother's. Besides being French, into heavy cream sauces and rare, undercooked duck with red cherries, her people are all reform. The least observant of all the Jews. They light *Shabbos* candles, and often eat milk and meat together at the same meal. On the same plates. Sometimes they have Christmas trees in their basements. With a six-pointed Star of David on the top evergreen branch.

It's exactly the same with her husband, Marvin. About stains and wrinkles, they are completely simpatico. So when she can't get the spots out by herself, I know how sick she really is. I start to count all the new spots. But I don't say a word to my father, Marvin, who walks around the apartment. Every night after he's finished working. Like it's perfectly natural. With a bottle of seltzer water mixed with ammonia trying to remove not only every spot she makes but also the accompanying smell. Which is sometimes worse than the spot itself. Good, white carpet absorbs odors like thick, soft cotton balls. Marvin wants to save the carpet from going way downhill.

Edith hates odors of any kind, especially body ones. One of the first words she teaches me is *houseatosis*. I never forget how to spell it. We walk around the house on Lynn Avenue sniffing. Corners. Toilets. The oblong cushions in the living room couch. The linen closet. Together we have a lot of fun. After they move in, the carpet never looks new again. Even though he bends down low from the knees and rubs extra hard. Every day. Back and forth. He keeps trying to rub out the spots after my mother dies. My sisters and I quit trying to get the spots out. For good. It's too exhausting. But Marvin never does. Quit trying. That's just his essential nature. An inborn quality that most people in Dayton find very endearing.

My favorite spot is what I identify as ethnic or culturally specific—Jewish American. Chunky peanut butter from a greasy-with-butter Lender's frozen then toasted poppyseed bagel. Growing up, I watch my father put a layer of peanut butter on his Lender's after he butters it with Fleischmann's one-hundred-percent corn oil margarine. And then I do the same. All of us, Judy, Jan, and Jyl, spend most of our lives following in our parents' footsteps. Even though Edith and Marvin never recognize these acute, tiny similarities. Edith has smaller feet than Marvin. Who has bigger feet than his father from Russia. "They are brothers," he tells me today. As if I didn't already know. "There are two of them. Muray and Marvin. Just like you girls. Their names both begin with the same letter, 'M.' The Lender brothers. It's a family business and they keep it that way. Do you know why they've been so successful, branching out into all those different flavors: onion, garlic, and pumpernickel? They trust each other. And it shows the way those boys do business." I nod. To Marvin Felman, Muray and Marvin Lender are a contemporary biblical parable. Timeless. Imbued with great meaning.

I don't believe him totally. It's a little after seven in the morning. We're watching the *Today* show and eating our toasted bagels. I'm home alone with Edith and Marvin. Visiting my mother because she's sick. I find it very hard to come home. He stresses this Lender's family point to me on more than one occasion. But I notice that as my mother gets sicker, my father gets more upset that none of his girls wants to go into the parking lot business. Eventually, he'll have to sell. Out for good. Marvin's not happy about the situation. He uses examples from history to reinforce the changing nature of the world today. For Jews. And everybody else.

He tells me that Jack Kennedy worked closely with his brothers. Especially Robert, who was his attorney general. Looking carefully out for his older brother, Jack, Robert astutely advised him on the developing civil rights situation in the South. Abortion and the separation of church and state. Which at the time had all the American Jews very worried. The Kennedy brothers ran the whole country like one big, extended family from Washington to Hyannis Port, from Camp David to Boston. And back again. Ted was in the Senate. The Kennedys are a lot like the Edgar J. Bronfmans in Toronto. Who travel back and forth regularly between the Middle East and North America. Marvin doesn't think hard liquor is a good business for Jews. And then there are the Baron de Rothschilds, who are all very close. All the men my father admires are brothers. Or sons. Who work with their fathers. My father's father is an orphan.

Marvin loves his big sister, Naomi, very much. She lives in New Mexico with the Marranos, the hidden, Catholic Jews. Who are expelled from Spain. Because they refuse to convert. According to the king's orders. Their descendants continue to light *Shabbos* candles in the dark in the basement. They are afraid of getting caught. As adults, whole years speed by, one after another in quick succession, before older sister Naomi and little brother Marvin see each other. After a while Marvin finally flies out to New Mexico for a short, twenty-four-hour visit. Every six months they talk on the phone. Marvin calls Naomi. By the end, he maintains the whole family. Connection. Single-handedly. The parking lots. The Eva Felman Apartments. His father. Edith. All of us. Judy, Jan, and Jyl. When Edith gets sick, Marvin is the tenuous link between us. And we know it.

I can't remember the last time Naomi sees her father, my grandfather. No one mentions this. After their expulsion, the Jews from Spain never go home again. It's been going on for so long the situation feels completely natural. To me and my sisters. Jews are expelled from almost every country we ever live in. Except Jamaica. And Cuba, which we leave quickly and voluntarily. I don't know when I first realized. That Naomi's absence is a big part of the family. Our collective history. That as Jews we never forget. With a separate identity. All its own. Marvin's more earnest this morning than usual. Maybe he's worried about Edith. But he won't ever say. Instead, he discusses and I listen. To his favorite topic, "The Jews made a big mistake." I'm looking down when he starts. Checking for more food spots. They're the worst to get out once they settle and dry.

It's not often that Marvin admits that either he or the Jews make a mistake. I sit up, stop listening to the *Today* show, and finally spot a new spot on the carpet. I resist the urge to pour my entire glass of water directly on what looks like milk—white on white. Removing spots has become an unconscious reflex. For my father, Judy, Jan, and me. We do it automatically. I say, "How so?" I'm asking Marvin about the Jews. Marvin is excited that I'm home visiting. He loves to explain Judaic history to any of his three daughters who will listen. To his wife/my mother. Or to anyone else, for that matter. My father should have been a rabbi. He's gifted, has so much to say; all he needs is a regular audience. He has the right kind of face: stern, very sincere, yet kind. He's handsome, which is unusual for a rabbi. And he still has all his hair. So does his father. We girls don't have to worry; we'll always have plenty of hair. Everywhere. Marvin has great, sensitive brown eyes with bushy, authentically furrowed brows. He's a deep man. To have for a father.

Edith is full of admiration for the depth of her husband's knowledge. And longs for her daughters to feel the same. "How do you know that?" she always asks him. A loving smile on her face. My mother is wheeled up to the table, as close as she can be without spilling her breakfast—scrambled eggs—on the carpet or scratching the veneer finish on the dining room table. That's been in the family for years. It's a heavy table. Passed down from generation to generation. Marvin and I sit on orange crushed-velvet. I can't tell if she's listening or dreaming. But she doesn't take her eyes off him. Marvin continues.

"In the beginning, when the Jews come to America,

they want to leave behind the old country. Each generation, myself included, encouraged their children to do better than their parents before them." Marvin nods at Edith. "To branch out and become professionals. Lawyers, doctors, heart surgeons, veterinarians. Atomic scientists and linguistic specialists. The children have to contribute something new and worthwhile to society. The Jews feel an obligation to the host country. And the parents," he's not finished, "including your mother and myself, do too good a job. Consequently, there's no one left to run the family businesses." My father is wiping his eyes with his handkerchief.

An ordinary conversation with Marvin often sounds more like the weekly Torah commentary. He shakes his head. Pauses for emphasis, points occasionally into the air, and then clears his throat to command your complete attention. I imagine him addressing the entire congregation of Bet Avraham. Where all the Felman girls celebrated our Bat Mitzvahs. And Edith planned the receptions. With bouquets of hot pink alstroemerias and deep red tulips from Amsterdam. My mother, the *rebbetzin*, is chewing her bagel. And keeping her eyes on her husband while he speaks. "You can see it right here in Dayton. The Levitt's dry cleaners, the Remick's scrap metal yard, and even the Schpinner's Great Scott supermarkets that the brothers started from scratch, selling door-to-door their mother Dora's homemade seedless dark rye bread.

"First they added jars of hot mustard that sold out

immediately. Then large dill pickles. But it was too much for the boys to carry door-to-door. So the Schpinner brothers saved every penny until they could afford to buy an old, ant-infested building that was a used-car dealership. Gutting the building, they turn it into the first Great Scott Supermarket. Eventually all those men had to sell outside the family. All that hard work. For nothing." Then my father the rabbi bows his furrowed brow and asks the congregation to rise for the *kaddish*, the mourner's prayer. How did the Lender Bagel brothers do it, I wonder? Working side by side for over fifty years. Both of them together. With their father. Every day. Nuclear Jewish families living in the Diaspora are a complete mystery to me.

My father works side by side with his father, my grandfather from Russia, his whole life. He says he wouldn't change a thing, not a single day. From hour to hour. I know he's not just talking about his father. He's talking about my mother's twelve years of Parkinson's. That starts early. Before she's even diagnosed. When she's fifty, he's fifty-two-and-a-half, and I'm twenty-five. She's sick at home on Lynn Avenue. And then later in the Eva Felman Apartments. Together, side by side, father and son work seven days a week, including *Shabbos*. They park cars; pick up cigarette butts, used condoms, double strength kleenex tissues, and all other trash; paint bright yellow stripes; plow the snow at 5:00 A.M. or earlier. Eventually, after much hard work, long hours, and many fights with the *goyisha* bankers, they buy the lots themselves. Slowly, gradually, like many immigrants before them, my father and his father, who is a little nervous, move into real estate and out of the physically exhausting business of parking cars. Station wagons, sedans, compacts. The Mustang is Marvin's favorite. My grandfather prefers the Lincoln Continental. Brand new. With red leather upholstery on the interior that he hand washes and towel dries himself. With his green garden hose.

By the time my father can take a real vacation to pray at the Wailing Wall in Jerusalem, play in the men's bridge tournament in Miami Beach, or see the red tulips next door to the Anne Frank House in Amsterdam in April, my mother's head aches nonstop. She doesn't say a word. No one knows how much her head hurts for over five years. Like a bomb, she tells me later. That keeps exploding over and over again. Inside a very small, dark cavity. And spreading outward until the whole body shakes. Uncontrollably. My father's mother, my grandmother Eva, works with her big boys taking the tickets at the front of the parking lots and making change for all the customers. Eva dies young. Before my Bat Mitzvah. Her breasts are full of tumorous lumps. Cancer. My mother's mother, Tessie—whose husband Alfred (my other grandfather) lives to eighty-five—dies young. So does my mother. None of the women in my family live past sixty-five. The men go on forever. Like Moses who lives to be one hundred and twenty. My grandfather is a hundred himself. The only thing he can't do is drive a car.

The Parkinson's gets really bad. Edith eats dinner at 4:00 in the afternoon, before the L-dopa wears off. And her body goes completely rigid. Marvin leaves work early all the time. To take his wife and his father out for dinner. Marvin works right below his father's apartment on the sixth floor of the Eva Felman Apartments. For years he plans it just this way. So he can be close to Edith in case she needs him. And his father. Edith is a great cook when we live on Lynn Avenue. I know my father misses eating at home, especially on *Shabbos*. She makes all his favorites: well-done brisket with the au jus on the side, noodle kugel and beet salad. We never discuss it. The Chinese restaurant on Salem Avenue out by the Jewish Community Center is the nicest to my mother. They have a special table for her and her wheelchair, my father, and his father.

A very good end location, not too far back. As if the maître d' wants Edith out of the way. And not too close to the door so that she's on display. They don't worry if she makes a mess of their beautiful handwoven rugs. Every month my father pays the dry cleaning bill. The bathrooms are spotless, and the women's restroom is big enough for a wheelchair. The Chinese understand my mother's predicament without my father saying a word. At the Peking Garden, Edith is royalty. Marvin's father is shown great respect. The Chinese and the

Jews revere their elders. And the owner, Mr. John Chen, and his wife, Susie, never suggest anything with pork to Marvin. Like wontons or pork fried rice. His dietary habits are understood. Marvin teaches his father what's good in Chinese restaurants: Chop suey. Egg fu yung. Chow mein with dry, crispy noodles.

Before they marry, my mother's favorite dish is sautéed jumbo butterfly shrimp in melted garlic butter. She orders it whenever she can. When she's nineteen, she gives up *treif*. For Marvin. For good. It's a good bargain. She never mentions butterfly shrimp again. He takes care of her for the rest of her entire life. The Jewish Home for the aged and the infirm is absolutely out of the question. For his father. And my mother. Not because it's an hour's drive away in Cincinnati. But because of Marvin. That's the way he is. He also makes sure all the tenants in the Eva Felman Apartments have downtown parking and wall-to-wall carpet. And he cleans the lobby himself, vacuuming and picking up the trash. Like at the parking lots. He doesn't want the building to be an embarrassment. To his dead mother. Or his father when he comes home at night.

My father's father's only daughter (my father's only sister), Aunt Naomi, doesn't work the lots. I hear that growing up she is overweight and not very attractive. Just Marvin and his parents. And none of Marvin's girls lives in Dayton. Like Naomi, we move away. After college Judy goes all the way to Port Hardy, British Columbia, in Canada where she has to row a boat out to the island in the monsoon season when the waters get too high to use the bridge. Like our real aunt—whom we don't see very much—Judy enjoys living with the native peoples of the land. Which she could also do with the Israelis and the Palestinians. If she ever wanted to. Jan goes off to the rural hills of Georgia to do volunteer work for the long, hot summers. Later she moves to Pittsburgh. Like Golda Meyerwitz, who changes her name to Meir. And leaves her mother and father in Milwaukee, Wisconsin. I begin to go by my Hebrew name, Giela, with a hard "G," and leave home for Kibbutz Gonen in the Galilee when I am seventeen. I am the first in my family to visit the Jewish homeland. Marvin always wants to go to Jerusalem but he has trouble leaving his father and the parking lots unattended.

Golda is still alive when I get to Israel. I hear her speak Hebrew to a bunch of American Jews, teenagers like myself. I plan to be gone a long time. Six months later, I return to the States because I can't stop eating. In the holy land. Chocolate-covered halvah with crushed pistachios, and black olives swirling in plates of fresh hummus, and smooth baba ghanoush. In Dayton, everything is frozen except the corn. Which grows on all the land all the way out to the airport. Marvin doesn't like vegetables. He likes iceberg lettuce with Wishbone Italian dressing. That's it for chlorophyll. I never come back to Dayton except to visit. My mother when she's sick. And even then, I don't come home enough. To see her. Or my grandfather. No one has to tell me. I already know. How much it hurts my father. Judy and Jan come home more often then I do. I know. I count every visit. Everybody else does too. Even though we never discuss the fact that we are each keeping track. Silently to ourselves. Of all our visits home to Edith. (And our orphaned grandfather from Russia.) My father counts too. Three years after Edith dies, Marvin asks me over the phone why I never came home. I'm not proud of myself. But Aunt Naomi doesn't come home either. Once she told me that the food in New Mexico is terrific. Everything's fresh. You can eat as much as you want. There's plenty to go around.

The one thing Edith does that surprises all of us is that she makes a lot of noise whenever she chews. She does this the whole time we are growing up. On Lynn Avenue. It's so unlike her. She's such a lady. And French. Even when she's sick with the Parkinson's that causes so much rigidity in the body. The illness never affects her ability to chew. Or her appetite. But at some point she can't smile any more. She loses control of all the muscles in her face. Until she has no expression. Left. Edith always has a smile on her face. Before she is sick. We, her daughters in America, learn to do the same. That way, all kinds of people everywhere are drawn to the Felman girls. Bagels are especially noisy. As food goes.

Although she definitely chews with her mouth tightly closed, just like she teaches us, we can still hear her chewing, grinding away with every bite. It is an unmistakable sound that I recognize instantly. She should do commercials for the Lender brothers. She prefers poppyseed. It doesn't make sense, her chewing so loud that the whole table can hear. We aren't ever allowed to talk and eat at the same time. Marvin is very quiet when he chews. Occasionally I hear his teeth click, but it's nothing like Edith when she chews. My father's father likes to click his false teeth together when he's done eating. That means it's time to clear his plate.

We have to swallow first. Everything. And then rinse with a quick sip of water. Running our tongues across our front teeth, checking to make sure that there isn't any ugly chopped spinach or kosher roast chicken caught in our molars. Our front teeth. Sitting together at Marvin's table we discuss current events—Vietnam, voting rights, and the new American movement Jews for Jesus. Marvin is against the war from the start. A lot of Jews are. While we discuss world affairs our teeth have to be perfectly clean. Toothpicks are absolutely forbidden. I use a toothpick at the table when I get older. I know it looks awful. But it reminds me of Edith and keeps the food out of my front teeth.

Eating with the Felmans is a delicate balance between actually enjoying the food and paying special attention to Edith's rules of order. We are not permitted to accidentally hit our straight white front teeth with our mother's silver spoons as we bring the food up to our mouths. Judy and Jan wear braces growing up. I don't. My teeth are born discolored but very straight. It isn't a problem with the drinking water. Like the entire neighborhood assumes. Or the polio vaccine we line up at the high school to take. By the time I come along, Edith runs out of calcium. It's that simple. Deprivation becomes a family theme. And a powerful cultural metaphor. I do not have poor dental hygiene. We floss after very meal. Later my female dentist talks me into off-white veneers. So my teeth look less discolored and more natural. Marvin is pleased and pays for the tooth coating. He pays for Judy and Jan's braces. All his life he wants everything to be fair and equal. I want to tell him that the smartest thing Jimmy Carter ever said before he had to leave office (because of the unfreed hostages) is that *life isn't fair*.

My family is noise sensitive. Neither Marvin nor Edith likes the clicking sound of the spoon against the teeth. I have to be careful when I eat that I don't crack my new shiny off-white veneers. We eat Chinese outside the house with gentiles and other people. We use chopsticks and chew with our mouths closed. We never talk with food in our mouths. I notice other people's food manners. Most people eat really fast, sit far away from the table like they have a plane to catch, and talk with all kinds of food in their mouths. Marvin says that he graduated *magna cum laude* from the Edith Jeanne Felman School of Training. Before he marries, by his own admission, his manners are more Russian in style, shoveling the food in quickly before it gets cold. After marriage to Edith, he switches over to the French side.

His father from Russia always wants to know where Marvin gets those fancy table manners. A knife is a knife. And a fork is just a fork.

Right now I'm nervous. I notice that I'm unconsciously but very lightly banging my teaspoon against my coffee cup. It makes a strange sound. Any minute someone's going to tell me to stop. Before I crack Edith's French Limoges coffee cup. And it breaks in half. But when Edith chews, she looks directly at you, as though she doesn't have a care in the world. And just what on earth, she wonders with those big, round brown eyes of hers, is bothering you. Because she's fine, enjoying her bagel and morning coffee. Black. No cream. Half & Half, or even skim milk, is fattening. Adding too many extra calories in an unnecessary way. All the Felmans drink their coffee black. It's nothing new. We always have. Kept kosher in Dayton. And watched our weight. Only Marvin, running around, parking cars seven days a week, waiting on all his girls and his father, doesn't ever have to count calories or pounds. He weighs the same as he does in the navy, which is only ten more pounds than when he was a Bar Mitzvah boy standing on the *bimah* with his father, fresh shaven and reading from the Torah. I've seen pictures. Women aren't allowed on the *bimah* for another twenty years.

The seventh floor Eva Felman Apartment is beautiful and doesn't smell when Edith and Marvin first move in. In the early stages, she isn't too sick to dust or vacuum. And hasn't started living in a wheelchair. The appliances. The furniture. Everything is modern and has such a nice, clean lemon scent. There's not a single spot. On the thick, white plush carpet. It's wonderful. Like living on the concierge floor of the Sheraton Towers. My father wants to start fresh. The living room is entirely white except for the orange crushed-velvet dining room chairs that she doesn't recover because they still look brand new. Edith hates to waste Marvin's hard-earned money. Besides if you brush it. Back and forth at least once a week. Orange velvet lasts forever.

Their bedroom is all white, with a shiny peach quilted bedspread. Gone is the lime-green-vegetable-and-giant-orange-flowered wallpaper that she puts up from floor to ceiling to match the carpet on Lynn Avenue. Edith likes atmosphere. In every room. In the home of my mythical childhood she uses wallpaper on the ceiling to create mood. The light switches and electric outlets are all papered to match the walls. So are the doorknobs. They're very hard to turn. My father's father hates wallpaper. Of any kind. It's for the *goyim*, he tells me. Polka dots. Stripes. Cats and dogs crawling up walls is enough to make a grown man sick to his stomach. In his own house.

In retrospect, Edith admits she makes a mistake about papering the sockets and the shower. Papered sockets are an electrical fire hazard. And in the shower, the wet paper ultimately cracks and doesn't look good. She puts a ladder in the tub by herself and takes the Elmer's Glue with her. Slowly, careful not to fall in the tub, she glues back the cracked orange-flowered wallpaper that always makes me dizzy in the shower. She has to preserve the atmosphere she works so hard to create. In the house on Lynn Avenue. That Marvin picks. He loves privacy. It's the last house on a dead end. And the used orange and green carpet is in excellent condition. Not many spots when they move in. At our end of the street it's very quiet. Except for the Millers' two gray schnauzers that bark nonstop. They don't jump; they bark. The schnauzers live next to the Schears, "Aunt" Betty and "Uncle" Bert.

When Edith's sick, my father has to put her in the tub himself and sponge her down with warm water and Johnson's baby soap because she can't do it for herself anymore. And her skin is so sensitive. My mother has a special light blue sponge. That she likes to fill with warm water and squeeze slowly down her back. Now my father does the squeezing. He's gentle, dripping water down my mother's back. Edith loves to bathe, to sit for hours in a steaming tub. With the door closed. My mother sits back and relaxes by herself. For almost an hour. When I'm little I sit on the toilet seat and watch her bathe. Sometimes I stand up and climb right into the tub with her. We wash each other's backs. Squeeze by squeeze. But when she's sick, she can't take a soothing bath alone. This upsets her. In my house, all the walls are painted. White. There is no wallpaper any-where in sight. I like it that way. I know if she were still alive, Edith would find it all a little bland. That's just one of the differences between us. Besides my preference for women.

Before the wheelchair there is the plunger. That my mother uses to walk. Around the apartment. But the problem with the plunger is that it sucks up. Everything. Which is what it's supposed to do. If you use it properly—what it's originally designed for. Flushing out stopped-up toilets. Not as an ersatz walking cane. The plunger is ordinary. An ancient relic my father keeps to remind himself just how far he's come. Left over from the parking lots. Marvin and his father used it to clean out the toilets that the customers always stopped up. Plain, unvarnished, smooth-sanded wood with a red rubber cup on the bottom. That sucks up the thick white carpet whenever my mother pushes down hard, to steady herself, get balanced, and walk forward. I watch Edith plunge around the apartment. Like Houdini, she lurches forward, as if she's going to fall off the skyscraper. Any minute. But she doesn't. At first. The plunger seems to work just fine. No one says a word. As if this is a perfectly normal use for a plunger.

I have no idea when the plunger becomes my mother's walking cane. One day, I hear from the nurse that Edith starts falling. Around the Eva Felman Apartments. The first all-electric heat and air conditioned units to come with parking in downtown Dayton. The hallways are wallpapered and carpeted in a luxurious red. Where you come out of the elevator on each floor,

Marvin hangs a big picture of a fancy French woman in a long dress and nice hat with a parasol in her hand. And petite white lace gloves. Good, solid Renoir reproductions. On every floor of the building. Whenever my grandfather travels from floor to floor and steps out of the elevator, he gets dizzy. My father, Marvin, dreams big. He has visions of how the world ought to be and what he wants to accomplish before he dies. It's a lot.

He wants his daughters to do the same. Have goals. Plan for the future with imagination and zest. But he doesn't understand. That it's always been different for his girls. Whom he loves very much. Each of us in our own, unique way. Edith can't hold on to her balance. This effects us, her three daughters. Very much. I don't really have the words to explain the situation to Marvin. From the minute she is diagnosed, Edith has trouble walking. Forward. And so do her daughters. For a long time Marvin has all the vision there is to have. In the entire Felman family.

That's the trouble with Parkinson's patients. One day they just start falling. And never stop. Falling. Edith breaks her hip in one of the falls. This throws her curvature of the spine off even more. She has to start wearing those ugly, black orthopedic shoes. My mother is such a stylish woman. From the day she is born. Her whole life. The left heel is six inches taller than the right heel. To even out the curvature and the broken hip. Finally my mother gives up completely: she stops walking and talking. Altogether. I think it is the heavy, black orthopedic shoes. They offend her sensibility and stick out. It's bad enough when all she can wear is aerobic shoes.

But Edith never stops having her hair done. In the wheelchair the nurse rolls her right up to the sink. One day my father begins to feed his wife. Who can't feed herself. For the last three years of her life. She just stops. Holding her silver spoon in her own hand. She can't open her hand, which is rigid in a fist. The L-dopa wears off sooner and sooner. The medicine used to last all day. If she's lucky, Edith has a couple of hours. To move her fingers. Marvin loves conversation. He never runs out of topics. This is remarkable. My father has enormous quantities of energy. Stored in reserve. For difficult times. Marvin picks up his wife's spoon—the one Jan wants—while he mentions something in the news. And then, as though it is the most natural thing in the world. He does it every day, like shaving. He brings the spoon right up to my mother's mouth. Which she opens slowly. By herself. The good thing about my father feeding my mother is that he doesn't make as big a mess as she does. The thick white carpet under the dining room table stays cleaner. Much longer.

It just happens. One day at a time. First she needs help getting dressed. Then bathing. And finally eating. Until Marvin has to stop eating and start feeding his wife. I find out he eats alone. Afterwards. A frozen Chef Boyardee pizza. Or popcorn from the microwave. In the beginning, I hardly notice the changes. When I'm home visiting. He just reaches up and wipes her mouth. With his cloth napkin. It's such a small gesture. Because Edith is fastidious. And doesn't like any crumbs or small food particles, especially scrambled eggs, to be anywhere but in her mouth. The gesture simply reminds me of how well these two people know each other. Like finishing each other's sentences. Marvin reaches up to touch Edith's lips. My mother. His wife. I watch. In silence. Wondering when she stops being able to wipe her own mouth. And what on earth is next.

We are a family in deep trouble. Only Marvin knows the depth of this trouble. Because he's the only one who sees Edith change. The daughters feel the change miles away. In Pittsburgh. Port Hardy, British Columbia. And Northampton, Massachusetts. But he sees it. Month by month. Week by week. Day after day. Until she's not the same person from one minute to the next. I know my father doesn't talk about it. Because he can't. If he started, he'd probably never stop. And he doesn't want us to either. Talk. We need to respect his silence. And his privacy. It's hard. He wants his girls to go on with our own lives. Dream big. Be more like him. With imagination and zest. We're young. And the rest of our many days stretch out before us. But what he doesn't know is that we can't. None of his girls. My sisters. Can go on with our lives. While she's sick. Only recently. I understand. The rigidity is contagious. For twelve years. Edith is his wife. Our mother. Only Marvin keeps moving. Forging ahead. Like all the other immigrants before him. Who learn English at night. And can never afford to look back. Have regrets. Or stop. To breathe. Even for a minute. Take a single day off. The silence is as thick as the plush white carpet. When it's new. Before the Tropicana. And the Folgers mountain-grown decaffeinated black coffee.

To me, my father is just like the Lender brothers, Muray and Marvin. After Edith dies. He keeps her in the family. And everyone else. All the different varieties. He never sells out. Ever. I wish we could talk about the family business. What's going to happen when Marvin's father dies. When Marvin dies. Because we're going to have to sell. Out. He knows this. Is true. All his hard work. And his father's hard work. He needs new carpet. For the apartment/his office. In Eva's hall-ways. None of Marvin's daughters can ever run the fam-ily business. Like he does. We would have to work to-gether. Like the Kennedy brothers. Or the Edgar J. Bronfmans. The Baron de Rothschilds spread out all across Europe. Marvin and his father. Side by side. Day by day. I couldn't make this story up if I tried. We don't even try. My sisters. I can't remember the last time I speak with Judy on the phone. Jan leaves me a message. Four weeks ago. It's been over two years since I've seen my sisters. The last time was at Edith's unveiling. I don't call Jan back. I don't know why. I don't even know how Aunt Naomi is doing in New Mexico. Or my mother's only sister. Shirley. Whom Edith used to talk to at least twice a week. Every week. Until she stopped talking.

Public Exposure

M Y MOTHER'S WHEELCHAIR is ancient. Big, bulky, the heavy metal kind that came out with the polio epidemic in the fifties. The wheels turn and the spikes shine. I see my own reflection going round and round. I am dizzy. My mother is the lucky, blessed, sacred symptom bearer who is chosen to absorb the entire neurological disorder and disintegration of the planet Earth in her one small, très petite female body. This apocalyptic, very Jewish vision came to me last week as I stared into a bowl of Rain Forest Crunch mixed with Nabisco Cheerios, toasted almond bits, and sun-dried California raisins. She has Parkinson's; the rest of us have the shakes. Her vocal chords have tightened up. She's living in an alternative, meditative state, conversing privately with the One On High *Baruch Ha Shem, Blessed Be The Holy One*. She stopped speaking years ago. "Scream," I want to say every time I look at her. "Just open your mouth and scream." My mother's eyes are big and brown. Even when I bend down low at the waist, eye contact is almost impossible to sustain.

My mother is unreachable. It's all that heavy metal. The wheels of her chair go round and round, slipping and sliding in between the cracks in the pavement. We used to hold hands, sitting in the front row of the avant-garde theatre in Yellow Springs. Afterwards we always shared a bottle of French chardonnay, lifting long-stemmed, gold-rimmed, hand-blown goblets and bending our heads together—forward as if in love—in that special girlish way. But now her hands are knots, her fingers do not bend. She doesn't like to be touched. When the L-dopa wears off, her whole body goes rigid. There is no such thing as relief. Or emancipation.

My father tells me that when they're on vacation, he leaves her in the car to get some milk. Her chair is too G-ddamn heavy to lift out of the trunk. He's only gone ten minutes. By mistake he locks his keys inside. She cannot open the car door to let him in. Her hands are in a palsied fist; she cannot bend her fingers. She is trapped inside, with the motor running and the air conditioning on. He will have to break into the car before she suffocates. The hot Florida sun reflecting through the window makes my mother sleepy. She cannot hear her husband rapping on the window with his wedding band. As she starts to doze her head jerks up and down. She has her seatbelt on. For protection.

In a panic he starts pounding on the glass. Her head

falls to the left. She is asleep. He is screaming, way too loud in the middle of the Boynton Beach parking lot, *Edith, open up! Open Up!* My father is hysterical. He doesn't want his wife to suffocate. I am holding my breath as he tells me the story. My father never asks for help.

In the background, a siren wails. A navy blue police car comes to a screeching halt. The cops start to arrest him. That's when I know we are living in the middle of a fast-paced TV docudrama. With his hands above his head, they pat him down. He says *Officer, this is a mistake, this woman is my wife. She's too sick to open the door.* My father is sweating; his face has lost its ruddy color. I can see this on HBO, in bright Technicolor. It would be great on Wednesday night. For almost thirty minutes she is locked in the car. *I need a coat hanger.* My father pleads with the officers. For the entire time she is sick, I never talk about my mother. What is there to say? I am the best supporting actress in a made-for-TV movie. About the family car. He has childproofed the doors. This is much too much to bear. For a single individual. At least my mother had her chair.

The exposure is complete. There are no more secrets. This is what I think when I take her to a public bathroom. Which is never accessible in spite of the picture-perfect mini-black wheelchair stenciled in the middle of the white swinging door that says *push*. When I "push" through the door I imagine that we become an instant Barbara Walters TV special on "Contemporary Mothers and Daughters." And as we roll into the restroom Barbara wants to know how I feel. She comes along for the ride. Only the stall is too small. For my mother's chair. I can't close the door or turn the chair around. The camera stops rolling. This isn't the story they came to shoot. But this is the true story of how I take my mother to the bathroom. In public.

With the door open, all the mothers and their children see right inside the stall. I wave to the crowd, flapping my mother's rigid arms up and down. The people stare back. I lift my mother out of her chair. She cannot hold onto me and her entire body falls against my chest. I can't believe how heavy this small woman is. *You weigh a ton*, I whisper in her ear. Then Barbara Walters tells me that she has a daughter too, with brown hair just like mine. Only they were never this close. Winking at my mother, whose eyes are almost closed, I say, *You have to work at it. It doesn't come naturally, this mother-daughter thing*. Barbara nods in understanding while I try to pull my mother's stretchpants down. I am panting, almost out of breath. The camera rolls again as I roll down my mother's underwear and push her onto the toilet seat.

When she's done, I flush the toilet with my left foot and wonder how I'm ever going to pick her up and put her back in the chair. I am hungry now. *Can you wipe yourself?* I say way too loud so that all the ladies in waiting and their preadolescent sons are sure to hear. I know she can't reach between her legs. Right this minute, a hot fudge mocha sundae would taste great with roasted pecans, finely chopped red and green maraschino cherries on top of melted miniature white buttered marshmallow puffs. The ice cream has to be from Friendly's. That's what I see in the air in front of me when I bend down to lift her up. And wipe her clean, spreading her buttocks gently as I wipe from the front to the back the way she always wiped me when I was a little girl. *You'll get sick the other way*, she used to say, wiping me away. Sometimes she misses the toilet seat. I remember the four-by-six-inch file card she taped above the light blue toilet seat at home. In black magic marker without smearing a word she had carefully printed: *If you sprinkle when you tinkle, then please be neat and wipe the seat.* I always wiped the seat. Before and afterwards.

When we got older she replaced the file card with a more professional hand-painted sign. In florid pink nail polish—right on the toilet seat—in bold capital letters she spelled out Flush! Whenever the pink paint cracked off, she repolished the seat herself, trying out dark reds and bright oranges to see if they had the same effect. It was Judy, my oldest sister, who never flushed on purpose. Nobody offers to help. They can see the perspiration on the back of my neck. Barbara Walters doesn't say a word. There isn't any room to bend down and wipe off the seat. I leave it wet, wishing I had a pen and paper so I could leave a note for the next in line. I feel the women watching; their eyes are big behind my back.

Will they actually put this segment on the air? All I have to do is pull up her pants and underwear at the same time and then we can roll right out. Backwards, we have to roll backwards. We can't turn around in here. I've never been fond of public bathrooms. They smell yellow and I never know whom I'll meet in there. The shiny metal wheels make me dizzy. We are rolling backwards.

When I'm home for a month in Dayton, Ohio, four Tuesdays in a row we go clothes shopping at Elder Berman's on the corner of Siebenthaler and Catalpa. I take her up to the third floor in the freight elevator because it is impossible to roll onto the always moving, shiny, gold-plated escalators that climb up a steep incline to Ladies' Lingerie on 2 and Misses' Dresses and Godiva Chocolates on 3. The freight elevator is in the back of the store. My mother slumps down low in her seat. If she slips out of the chair I'll run right over her sick female body. As I wheel her in, I see the gap between the floor and the elevator. She hates the cracks in the pavement. She feels every bump, just like the princess and the tiny, hard green pea underneath one hundred mattresses. I wish I could lift the whole chair up over the gap, but I can't. It's too heavy. I can barely push it over to the other side. My mother is so sensitive. And so am I. Sensitive.

The door to the lift is a manual gate. The iron bar sticks when I close it. I'm not sure I'll be able to open the gate. I'm sure I've locked us in. I shudder at the image in my head. For the rest of my life I'll be stuck in Dayton, Ohio, riding up and down in Elder Berman's freight elevator at the back of the store. My mother starts to cry. It's dark in here. I need water. My mouth is dry. I'll choke if we don't get out soon. We stop on the second floor. A store employee is standing next to three huge racks of women's sports ensembles he wants to wheel in. He's impatient, but I can't get the gate un-locked. There isn't any air. I stare at the clothes, seeing if there's anything I'd like to try on. "It's stuck," I say. I don't want to let him in. This is the only time I get to be alone with Edith without the nurse. There's one outfit that looks like my type. Black leggings with a matching black turtleneck. A little hot for the summer. Then I spot a black T-shirt with a scooped-out neck. I'd look great in that. Scoop necks show off my collarbone and make me a lesbian with hetero sex appeal. I can wear it at Friendly's, in the corner booth as I eat my hot fudge mocha sundae with red and green maraschino cherries chopped into small, bite-size pieces.

"It always jams from inside," he says. "You have to press really hard on the latch and even pound it a little." With great reluctance, I follow his instructions. The gate slides open and he slides the racks across the gap, bumping right into my mother in her chair. He pre-tends he doesn't see her sitting there. I have to lift the brake lever before I can move the chair to the left so there's room for all of us and the clothes. I imagine lift-ing the brake lever permanently, never locking it in place again. Rolling, rolling. We are rolling forward off the edge. Rolling. Rolling. Off the edge for good. The leggings come in lots of colors: orange, lime green, and sea blue, purple, fuchsia, and milk chocolate. We're all going to suffocate, pushed up against the wall, behind layers of one-hundred-percent cotton made in Taiwan. I swallow and pat my mother's head, which is soaking. Her body is rigid underneath my touch. It will be impossible to try clothes on, to lift her hands above her head. When we reach the third floor, I am exhausted. I do not understand how it came to this. My mother is asleep. Or dead and gone from me forever. I do not want to be a motherless child.

I am the exact same size as my mother, five-feet-one-and-a-half-inches tall, size 5–6 petite if we're wearing Liz Claiborne, 7–8 if we're wearing Isaac Mizrahi, whom my mother prefers because of his Hebrew name, which means *east*, as in Jerusalem the City of Golden Peace. We like to wear the sacred city on our backs. All the saleswomen are busy and so I go through the racks as fast as I can. Trying to engage my mother in the process—get her excited about the new summer pastels. Only we both hate pastels which are all the craze at the moment. Pinks and blues. Egg whites and awfully bright sunflower yellows. My eyes hurt. The colors remind us both of Easter eggs; we roll our eyes together, rejecting outright the current fashion trends. For a minute it's like old times, before the diagnosis. I see the waiter at the Gold Coin Cafe opening a tall, green bottle of my favorite French chardonnay. We always used to sit in the corner booth, under the fake Picasso from his Blue Period, sip our dry white wine with just a hint of oak, and talk about our purchases—what we're planning to return. Tomorrow. Only tomorrow never was.

I go to the Le Sport sales rack, right next to Misses' Dresses and Godiva Chocolates, and leave my mother, her head drooping to the left, sitting alone by the jewelry counter. I grab as many pullover tops and stretchpants as I can. Then I walk over to dump them in her lap. In the fifteen seconds it takes me to lift the brake lever and turn the chair around, I make a calculated decision. I run as fast as I can. Pushing my mother in her wheelchair I run back to the freight elevator screaming, "Out of my way, my mother's going to be sick. Any minute! Out of my way!" All the shoppers freeze instantly, moving to the left side of the aisle, just like when the ambulance zooms down the center of the street and all the cars pull over. Fast. Only the cars don't pull over anymore. They just stop. In the middle of the road. And people stare. Wondering who's dying now. Or whose body is burning, trapped under an overturned exploding '85 Chevy wagon.

On the first floor, I unlock the gate and scream again. Louder. Stronger. "Out of my way . . ." until we are all the way out of Elder Berman's department store. Rolling out into the parking lot. I never look back. Now it's me who's on fire from the inside out. Trapped underneath the burning flame of mother loss. At home, I smile in horror in the mirror. All the clothes piled high in my mother's lap fit perfectly. All the clothes that we stole. Together, like a couple of *gonifs*. Jewish thieves stealing from the *goyim*. Finally what they always say comes true. Yes, we stole the merchandise and wore it anyway. We adore our brand-new stolen clothes. We can never get enough.

For an entire year after she dies, my father keeps my mother's heavy metal wheelchair in the trunk of the car, where he always kept it when she was alive and they went out for a drive. Now I go for a ride with him not knowing that the chair is in the trunk. I sit where my mother used to sit slumped over in the front seat with her seatbelt on. We're on our way to Friendly's to taste the Jubilee Roll. I am wearing a black T-shirt with a scooped-out neck and I am looking forward to the combination of flavors, strawberry next to malted chocolate almond next to French vanilla with fudge ripples, all rolled in pistachio nut bits and glazed in Swiss butterscotch—that's the Jubilee part. My collarbone is exposed. The street has a lot of potholes. My father swerves around them, but we hit the largest one head on. And then I hear the thud from the back of the car. I hear the thud again on our way out of the pothole. My whole body jerks forward. The shoulder strap keeps me from banging my head and always kept my mother from banging hers.

My father says, looking straight ahead at the road,

"It's nothing, it's your mother, her chair." I don't say a word; it's been nearly twelve months since she died. My mother is still alive, groaning at every bump from inside the trunk of the big blue Chevy. "Her chair is too G-ddamn heavy," he says, turning into Friendly's on North Main Street. My mother is locked in the car. She is fighting for air. I develop a severe dislike for the trunks of cars. So severe that I avoid all contact with them. For months now, I haven't opened the trunk of my own car; I pile all my stuff in the backseat. I'm afraid she's curled up in the trunk. Her body rigid from the Parkinson's. She can't even knock on the inside, make a noise, let someone know she's there, buried alive in the back with all the equipment to change the right front totally deflated Firestone tire.

Everywhere I go wheelchairs follow me: in the bathroom at Logan Airport, at the check-out counter at Stop & Shop, and in the waiting room of my dentist's office. At the fruit stand on my way home, fresh-picked native strawberries are the weekly special for the whole month of June. But I don't pull over as I drive by. Underneath the umbrella, in the hot summer sun, the woman selling all the fruit sits in a wheelchair. The big, bulky heavy metal kind. I press the gas pedal and zoom by. I smell polio and Parkinson's. Fresh dew, hanging in the air. I love fresh strawberries but I don't eat them anymore.

I am in a hurry picking up my newspaper. As I turn to leave the State Street Market, I feel something heavy on my foot. The woman behind me at the checkout counter is rolling her wheelchair over my left foot. Backwards and forwards. When she apologizes, I don't even nod, but I notice that she is about to roll over my right foot as she tries to get closer to the counter. With all her groceries piled high in her lap. The milk is about to drop on the floor, followed by the Tropicana Grove-stand orange juice. If the carton breaks and sprays my legs and ankles, then I'll be really sticky until I can get home and sponge off the juice. She spills the juice all over me. Before I can get out of the way. My foot is caught under the wheel. Sweet, sticky, fresh-squeezed Tropicana gushes out everywhere, all over my small, très petite female body.

My mother is following me around. I am dizzy all the time. Right after she dies, I go to Florida, to Boynton Beach, where my father used to take her for a rest. I stare at the parking lot, where she nearly suffocated. Later, walking on the beach, I look up. Something big and bulky is moving toward me. Under the hot Florida sun, a gigantic soft leather sitting-up chair with pillows, perched high up on all-terrain wheels, is coming at me. A wheelchair for the beach. My mother always loved the beach at sunset when the tide was low. The entire nuclear family is out walking. The mother is the one in the chair. She is alert, smiling into the sea breeze. Her kids, two girls and a boy, skip alongside the chair, trying to keep up. Together. Under the sun, next to the water.

At dusk they make a beautiful Kodak portrait with the Atlantic lapping in the background. The only thing missing is the long-haired golden retriever jumping up and down.

I don't know why my mother had such an outdated wheelchair. Or why my father never got her an electric one, or at least a lightweight model. Instead, when she dies, we are all exhausted from pushing, pushing that G-ddamn heavy metal chair around in public. For years we are exhausted. Because my father insisted on taking her out. He didn't ever want his wife—my mother—to be housebound, locked inside, even when he went out for the milk.

Whenever I travel, I arrive early at the airport. On purpose. I like relaxing before boarding the plane. I have developed a routine. I look around the ticket counter, knowing exactly what I'm looking for. Usually there's a wheelchair in the back of the counter. I always leave enough time before my flight to walk up behind the counter and just sit down in the chair. I look around at all the people, imagining the world from my mother's point of view. Everything is cut in half. There are only children's faces at this level. And dogs and midgets. No adults. The children stare back. Before I know what's happening, I put my purse in my lap, lift the brake lever up, and roll out from behind the counter. I'm rolling. Rolling backwards. Off the edge. I hate wheelchairs.

I'm rolling. Rolling. Backwards. Until they have to carry me on board. For the rest of my life, I am carried on board before I fly. When we land, I stand up and walk off the plane with all the other passengers. But whenever I travel, I arrive early at the airport. On purpose. And I roll backwards. For the rest of my life.

Foreign Matter

T OWARD THE END of her life. Before she stops
   talking. Edith changes her mind. She no longer
believes in abortion. I am horrified. Edith has three
daughters.

She tells me. She could never have one. *It's a very
personal decision.* I tell her *fine. If you're against abortion, don't have one.* This is my favorite bumper sticker.
She shakes her head. Edith cries a lot with the Parkinson's. It's hard to know. If the cries are real tears. Full of
grief. And pain. Or just a spastic response. From a brain
that no longer manufactures the chemical dopamine.
Which controls the flow of emotions to the nervous system. She's talking about me. Judy and Jan. Her daughters. Our bodies. She tells me I take everything too personally. *Everything is not always about you, Jyl.* Which
is basically the problem for the Felman girls. Since the
moment we are born.

President Bush is against the use of fetal tissue. He's

afraid. That using fetal tissue for scientific purposes will encourage abortion. I never trust Bush. Who lies about the Iran-Contra deal. (And having an affair.) Or his wife, Barbara, who doesn't speak out about being proabortion until after Bush is defeated. And they're safely back home. Redecorating Texas. As First Lady, Barbara tries to bring back Jackie Kennedy's famous faux pearls. With the silver art deco style clasp. But Barbara's neck is too thick. For such an elegant look. When I am thirty-four. (Four-and-a-half years before Edith dies.) There is a medical breakthrough concerning the transfer of fetal tissue from aborted fetuses into the brains of Parkinson's patients. It's the first real hope.

Technically speaking. The placenta from a daughter's stomach could be implanted into the mother's brain. To save the mother's life. I think of Edith. And hate George Bush. The permanent reversal of all her acute debilitation. Is possible. A nightmare becomes a fleeting dream. Even the Talmud agrees. In rare circumstances *One life can be sacrificed to preserve another.* After years of being prochoice, a single 20/20 news broadcast, and a few outrageous words from the president, Edith becomes prolife. And so does Marvin. There's nothing left to discuss. It's not just semantics. We, the daughters, feel betrayed. Edith and Marvin see it differently. Of course. A daughter could save a mother's life. If only she is given the chance. To be her true self. One thing that I learn from Edith. Over and over again. Is that everything is related. Complete non sequiturs. Ultimately prove to be connected. Like the survivors of the Holocaust. Who later become Jewish psychoanalysts (in the tradition of Sigmund Freud). And vehemently renounce homosexuality as a disease of degeneracy. The Nazis fondle each other. They're bored in the camps; there is a slowdown in the ovens. And. To relieve the pressure. The guards fuck in the ass. Right in front of the prisoners. So how can Jewish doctors in the twentieth century. Ever be pro gay rights? Their imaginations are haunted.

To Edith. I am deeply connected.

My mother does not have the lifesaving surgery. In my mind fetal tissue is never the same again. She refuses the transfer of the placenta. Marvin refuses to discuss it. Edith's sister, Shirley, is a nurse. A big shot in the New York medical establishment. She has a Ph.D. Doctor of Nursing. Aunt Shirley wants to try anything that will save her sister. From silence. Life in a wheelchair. And paralysis. Shirley eats *treif*. In front of Marvin. For years. And lovingly encourages her children to eat whatever they want. Whenever our families are together in a restaurant. Everyone makes fun of Marvin. By mixing milk and meat together. This is the melting pot.

When I go to New York to visit, my mother's sister constantly tries to get me to taste all the rich, exotic delicacies swimming on the floor of the ocean: blackened sea scallops served on a bed of fresh linguine with fresh arugula sautéed in cilantro; chilled oysters on the half shell drenched in cognac. Escargots in butter, garlic, ground pepper, and fresh pesto. Baby prawns. From the Atlantic. Extra large. Jumbo shrimp: grilled or lightly battered tempura style, dipped in sweet and sour sauce that you eat with your fingers.

According to the laws of *kashrut*, eating is a sacred act. A Jew should not be a glutton at the table. Which is an altar. To life. Dr. Nurse, Aunt Shirley, eats octopus. All those legs, spread out in a perfect pin wheel on a blue ceramic plate. She tells me are a rare luxury. Completely delicious. She teases me: *You don't know what you're missing.* Marvin and Aunt Shirley never get along. Oil. And water. They pretend. To mix. As long as Edith is alive. Family is important.

On Lynn Avenue. We have rules about what we can eat and what we can't eat. Marvin tries to balance living in America with the conflicting interest of maintaining our cultural and religious heritage. In a secular world my father feels strongly that the spiritual life of the Jewish people is at risk. Once we set foot on Ellis Island. Marvin devises a plan. Edith wholeheartedly concurs. (She says) *A good relationship demands teamwork. Unanimity. And a united front.* Only in the Felman family. The daughters have no vote. Democracy is limited. To the clean, kosher hands of a powerful few.

We are the lucky beneficiaries. Edith says. Of a well-thought-out plan. About how to grow up in Dayton, Ohio, USA. Marvin disdains those who assimilate. He says he doesn't mind. Being different. (Neither do I.)

Intermarriage. Of any kind. Is out. (All my future girl-friends are Jewish.) Judy develops an overt fondness for gentiles. And an insatiable appetite. For big shoulders and blonde hair. Basketball and football stars. Quarter-backs. Forwards. Point guards.

Jan prefers intellectuals. Doctors of psychiatry. Law professors. Symphony conductors. Ivory chess players. According to Marvin the rules are as follows: *We are allowed to go out with gentiles to school functions. Only. With Jewish men we can go anywhere. We want. Within city limits.* We can't drive to Cincinnati. To see the Red Sox. That's going too far. Away from home. According to Marvin's stipulations.

All public high school athletic events. Hold unique potential. Judy becomes a budding sports fanatic. Other, specifically social events: proms, homecoming, the Fall Ball, Winter Wonderland, Spring Fantasy. The Easter Hop. Are also ripe with possibility. Judy learns to dance. The Twist. Other outings are more compli-cated. If the function is merely school related. It doesn't count. Ironically. There *aren't* a lot of places in Dayton, Ohio, to go with a Jewish date. (Just the opposite of Marvin's well-calibrated plan.) The movies. Friendly's restaurant for a hot fudge sundae with chopped pe-cans. Bowling.

I go to see Diana Ross and the Supremes change outfits and wigs after every song. *Stop. In the name of love*... With Steven Wasserman, Mark Stein, and Deb-orah Sugarman. *Before you break my heart* ... All adolescent American Jews. Girls. And Boys. *Think it ooooover....* The event is at the University of Dayton—a Catholic school where Lew Alcindor changes his name to Kareem Abdul-Jabbar. But the Supremes are not considered a school function. See how complicated it is. Minute details. Circumscribed minutely by Marvin. Who worries all the time. About his girls. And.

Who tries so hard. But he is. In the end. My father. Totally mystified. And unprepared, as his father is before him. To have a daughter. Instead of sons. To raise three Jewish girls in the Diaspora. He doesn't understand. The simplest mathematical equation: That which is absolutely forbidden. Is ultimately craved. Forever and ever. And that goes for all kinds of shellfish. Fresh. Or frozen. Birth control pills. Diaphragms: the Lippes loop. Pancetta: pink, thin-sliced Italian ham. *Milchig* and *fleishig* together. On the same blue ceramic plate. Broken hymens. Penetration. And sex. Before and outside marriage. With men. Gentiles. And women. If one of the daughters happens to be gay. As I am. Circumcision is not a problem. (Talmudically, the uncircumcised penis is just another kind of *treif*. And of course forbidden.)

Growing up. Edith's kitchen is kosher. Milk and meat are never eaten together. Which means a Jew can't have blue cheese salad dressing on her iceberg lettuce and two grilled lamp chops with mint jelly. At the same time. It's an ancient law. That has deep meaning. For some Jews. And Marvin. Two sets of dishes. Take up a lot of Edith's shelf space. My mother loves to shop at Macy's. When she's visiting Shirley in New York. For new china. That she has sent to Dayton. Marvin buys her all the dishes she wants. The patterns change seasonally. Edith has a large plate collection.

No pork anywhere in sight in the Felman household. According to Marvin's plan. We can eat whatever we want. Shellfish. Blue cheese dressing and lamb chops, together. On the same plate. When we eat out. Which starts happening when I am eight. Jan is ten. And Judy, twelve. The first place Marvin takes us. In the car. Is all the way down Salem Avenue. Straight to the Golden Arches. Edith loves picnics. She's in the front seat. We girls are in our assigned positions. In the back. In descending birth order. We're on our way home from religious school: Moses. Mount Sinai. The Old Testament.

It's 1962. (One year before Sandy Koufax wins the World Series.) Dayton is a test town for new products. We are middle America. Judy, Jan, and Jyl are stuck. In the middle. Of the past and the present. Public school. Hebrew School. We attend both. The Felman girls are in class six out of seven days of the week. 8:00 A.M. until 7:00 P.M. Excluding extracurricular activities. Highly motivated by the struggles of those who come before us, we follow the rules. And forge diligently ahead. My father's father has to leave school in the third grade. To sell newspapers on the street corner.

McDonald's comes to Dayton. French fries from

real Idaho potatoes. And double cheeseburgers. That Marvin refuses to eat. Milk and meat together. I watch. In awe. The very first time. My oldest sister Judy orders a double cheeseburger on a toasted, buttered sesame bun smothered in lettuce, tomato, mayo, mustard, and ketchup. Onions. Large crispy fries. A mocha *milk* shake. I'm too young to fully appreciate. The permanent, lasting, long-term significance of the ground - beef - sandwich - on - a - buttered - bun - with - melted-oozing-everywhere-cheese that my sister Judy orders. This is just the beginning. Of a fight that escalates. Out of proportion. Bigger and bigger. On and on.

Edith, Marvin, and I order square fish fillets. Frozen scrod with tartar sauce. Instantly. The borders are drawn. When Jan sides with Judy. And orders a double cheeseburger with all that oozing, melting cheese. Instead of a square frozen fish fillet. The family begins to split. In the car. Silently. At the Golden Arches. Slowly at first. Apple turnovers aren't introduced for another two years. Not until McDonald's realizes they have to offer dessert. In the Midwest. We eat dessert. Apple pie. Chocolate cake. Edith's homemade peanut butter cookies. Marvin pulls out of the parking lot quickly. The Golden Arches—symbol of all that's good in America—fade into the background. The family outing is halted abruptly when Judy says the cheeseburger on the buttered toasted bun tastes great. "Does anybody want a bite?" I shake my head. No.

My father's rules are simple. Inside the Felman

house, everything is kosher. Outside, he will continue to observe the laws of *kashrut* to the best of his ability. As does his wife Edith. But the girls—this is his big concession—can eat whatever we want: lobster Newburg, baked stuffed shrimp, veal parmigiana. Scallops Diane. Diane herself. Beyond the pale of Lynn Avenue. In secular, agnostic, hedonistic, narcissistic society, anything that we want goes into our mouths, landing in the middle of our plump little stomachs. I don't really believe him. There will be consequences. I am sure. Severe repercussions. Judy orders the first cheeseburger. Which requires a lot of internal chutzpah. Built up over a very long time. That I come to respect deeply. I regret my own refusal to taste even one small bite. That could have changed permanently the misalignment.

Loyalty is a central controlling metaphor. For Jews everywhere. Individuality is not rewarded. We are a communal people. Who miraculously establish Degania, the first kibbutz. Collective living in Palestine in the 1920s. In the face of great adversity, we act as one big family. That's why everyone thinks we're so clannish. We do. Stick together. It's almost impossible to separate the placenta from the womb. On kibbutz, all fetal tissue is precious. Since the founding of the Jewish State. Nation (re)building depends on the rigid cohesion of future generations. And the lack of all conscientious objectors.

Simultaneously. The umbilical cord in America is often wrapped around the baby's neck. Suffocation is a culturally specific medical condition resulting from grave historical circumstances that occur in this century in another part of the world. Consequently. Separation is a big theme. With the Felmans, each daughter goes about it differently. Judy and I aren't finished yet. We're in our late and early forties. Jan marries. With slight variations, modifications, and incremental improvements. She recreates urban, nuclear Jewish family life in Pittsburgh. We have no role models. Both our parents, Edith and Marvin, never actually leave home. Or say good-bye to their own mother and father. They are the "good" offspring. An Israeli who leaves home for a better, safer, richer life in the Diaspora is a disgrace. To the whole country. (And to Jews everywhere.)

Edith and Marvin have one sibling apiece. The "bad" offspring. Leave home. Seek their fortune. Never to return again. It is impossible for everyone to be good at the same time. My parents' siblings marry. Move away. Edith and Marvin remain behind. Where does that leave us? The daughters. When Edith gets sick. None of us moves back home to take care of our mother. Technically speaking. I could save my mother's life if she wasn't opposed to abortion. But it never even comes up. Instead we each go down a different road. That begins with Marvin's house rules. Doesn't Edith know. That rigidity kills all desire to move forward. And is the root cause of bunions. On your feet.

The second time foreign matter enters a Felman girl's esophagus. Via her large, sensuous mouth. It happens in a truly big way. And the family ends up. Eating the whole meal. In silence. Which is unusual. Because we always discuss current events. List what happens. Around the dinner table. Day by day. Hour by hour. In the '60s, we have a lot to talk about. At mealtime. All the assassinations: Medgar, Martin, Malcolm, John, and Bobby. Philip Roth's anti-Semitic imagination. In *Good-bye Columbus*. Splashed across the screen. For all the *goyim* to see. Us exposed. Marvin is furious. The Six-Day War (Israel against all Arabs everywhere). The disappointing fall of Saigon. Lenny Bruce's foul mouth. Koufax's refusal to play baseball on the High Holidays. (In America. He makes us very proud.)

We never stop talking. About Ed Sullivan, the Beatles, and long brown hair on grown men. Until the moment Judy and Jan order shrimp. Foreign matter. I know this is a test even though nobody says a thing. I don't think Marvin ever expected any of his daughters to actually eat shellfish. In front of him. At the same table. (Cheeseburgers aren't as bad as shrimp.) Those little scavengers that crawl all over the ocean floor remind him of the Nazis. Eating their babies one by one. Edith doesn't say a word. She feigns indifference. Fake *goyisha* nonchalance. We're eating Chinese.

When Judy and Jan order the butterfly shrimp off the pu-pu platter. I am caught. Right in the middle. If I don't immediately dip the butterfly shrimp into the duck sauce I am a traitor to my sisters. It's lonely being the favorite. And if I do dip the shellfish into the sweet

CRAVINGS

and sour sauce, my allegiance to Marvin and Edith is placed in severe jeopardy. Everything is related. Years later, I understand why I never eat the shrimp. I am saving myself for my first glorious woman lover. In melted butter. Crushed garlic. Fresh ground pepper.

In other Jewish families, loyalty doesn't always play out around food. (Sex, non-Jews, and lesbians.) But with the Felmans. Food is the way we show love. And disapproval. What we eat. And don't eat. Fat. Thin. Good. Bad. Up. Down. In. Out. Until Edith dies and I am almost forty, I do not eat *treif*. Or date non-Jewish men. I never have an abortion. How could I? Throw away all that lifesaving placenta? Just the thought. Makes me gag. Maintaining autonomy within the intimacy of the nuclear ethnic family. Is tricky. And requires much agility. Plus great dexterity.

Growing up I discover that the rigidity is contagious. Judy and Jan fight back. I watch from the sidelines. As my sisters grow to despise me. Everything Jewish is wonderful. Marvin, Edith, and I become a kosher triumvirate. We go everywhere. Together. Florida. Kentucky. Cincinnati. We light *Shabbos* candles wherever we go. I am filled with love. For my people. And my parents. When Edith's feet hurt her. I cannot find shoes to fit my own. Two feet. I develop huge, ugly, bulging bunions that match my mother's perfectly.

That's why. After depriving myself for years. And being Marvin's Jewish American kosher princess. And a very good little girl. (Except for the secret fact. That

158

from a very early age I enjoy putting my hands down the pants of other little nice Jewish girls.) When Edith dies. I start after many long years of respect for Marvin to eat shrimp. Slowly at first. Nervous. About all the loyalty issues. But I can't stop laughing at how good, how absolutely delicious New Orleans baked barbecue shrimp is. I make a huge scientific discovery. A lifesaving breakthrough. That includes: A ton of crushed garlic. A pound of melted butter. The juice of six succulent lemons squeezed gently over the jumbo scavengers. An entire four-ounce bottle of extra virgin olive oil flown in from Greece. Pepper. Worcestershire sauce. And a splash of Tabasco. All baked at 350 degrees for thirty very hot minutes.

Edith loves melted butter. On top of anything. New Orleans baked barbecue shrimp is my girlfriend Lauren's best dish. That she makes for me on our second date. She's Jewish too. Only keeping kosher has a different meaning for Lauren. More symbolic. Than literal. Lauren doesn't know Marvin. Who codifies his own highly specialized way of life. And puts it on the bookshelf between the Talmud and the great literary works of Maimonides, a famous Jewish philosopher. I tell myself. That I have to eat the shrimp. For my own good. Before it's too late.

Edith is dead. Half my life is over. I decide. Once and for all. To live my life. Not in my father's shadow. This is difficult. I spend years memorizing. All the rules. For Jewish survival. In America. Everything works fine. I love Marvin. And am devoted to both my parents. Until I fall madly, passionately, erotically, intellectually, delightfully, publicly in love. With a woman. And put her foreign matter in my mouth. And never take it out. Again. Because the taste of a woman is spectacular. About homosexuality. Marvin has no rules. Not a single codification on this burning, blazing social issue. (In the Five Books of Moses, sex between men is outlawed, while lesbians are nonexistent.) It simply never occurs to him. That any of his three beautiful, food-phobic-fanatic daughters. Might grow up to be gay. Of course. If it doesn't enter Marvin's mind. Then same-sex love never flashes across Edith's either. Although premarital sex is expressly forbidden in the house rules. Homosexuality lacks definition. By Marvin.

The problem with rules. Is you have to know when to follow them. And when to break them. Like sitting down at Woolworth's lunch counter. On the *whites only* side. Or taking a drink from the fountain of forbidden water. Because you're thirsty. From years of dehydration. Edith and Marvin. Never do.

At the end of my mother's life. There is a *true* scientific breakthrough. Not a metaphorical one. Concerning the cerebral tissue of a pig's brain. That is transplanted into the brain of a man with Parkinson's. This is a cause célèbre. Finally. An alternative to the surgical implantation of human fetal tissue is found. And an end to all my mother's awful debilitation is possible. I read an Associated Press account: "Previous attempts at cross-species transplants to cure human ills have failed. However, doctors say they believe there is a good chance this one will succeed, in part because the body's immune system defenses are weaker in the brain and thus less likely to reject foreign matter."

Of course Aunt Shirley, who eats *treif* (in front of Marvin), wants Edith to have the breakthrough surgery. Immediately. Edith keeps kosher. No human fetal tissue ever enters her system. Judy and Jan eat chilled baby shrimp in long-stemmed parfait dishes. To lose weight, to have a life of their own. Jyl is a lesbian. Which saves her from a life of paralysis. She learns after many years. To eat shrimp. But she never tells Marvin. Or Judy and Jan. What she puts in her mouth. And just how good it tastes.

Edith never has the pig surgery. She hates experiments. The mice always end up dead or with cancer. The Nazis experimented. On the Jews. For scientific purposes. Everything is related. I keep wondering if the brain tissue of a slovenly pig could, should be used to save my mother's life. I save the newspaper article. Reading it over and over. The last paragraph says, "Between 500,000 and 1.5 million Americans have Parkinson's disease, which causes muscle rigidity and tremors and makes movement difficult. The disease results from the death of specialized brain cells that make dopamine, a chemical the brain uses to communicate."

What the article never discusses. Is that Jews get

Parkinson's more than any other sociocultural group. (An astonishingly high percentage of the not quite six million Jews in America are paralyzed.) I learn this important fact from the writing of Dr. Oliver Sacks. He writes wonderful books about L-dopa, the wonder drug that releases all the rigidity. In Jews. Who suffer from Parkinson's. (Robin Williams plays the Jewish Dr. Oliver Sacks in the movie version called *Awakening*. Which makes me cry incessantly for hours.) In America, we have to learn how to mix and melt. Or we'll never survive. The next millennium. I plan to donate my organs to science. To anyone who will take them into their system. The foreign organs of a Jewish lesbian vegetarian chicken writer. Given the chance, I could save a life. Or two.

When Edith dies. Marvin marries again. After almost forty-five years of marriage to the same woman. My father starts over. A year later. His new wife gives up shrimp for her new husband. What is it about my father that makes women's taste buds go haywire? Marvin and the new Mrs. Felman live happily ever after. In Dayton, Ohio, USA. Mrs. Marvin Felman has the rabbi over to her house to bury all her cooking pots in Pearl S. Buck's good clean earth and to kosher her kitchen with Hebrew blessings. Before Marvin moves in. *After* they exchange vows and stand under the *chupah*. Not before. The odd thing is. The new Mrs. Felman has a daughter who is a lesbian. And loves shellfish. So there are two of us from Dayton, Ohio.

My father assures me that he follows his own rules. He moves in. Only after the kitchen is thoroughly koshered. The question I have is whether or not. The Nobel Prize laureate and Holocaust survivor Elie Wiesel, who defies *goyisha* gravity and keeps strictly kosher while interned for years in Auschwitz, would have the pig surgery. If he ever gets Parkinson's and is unable due to all the rigidity to write all his Holocaust memoirs for the rest of the world to read. I'm not sure what Wiesel would do. Like Edith, he is a French Jew. He writes his true-life stories in his birth language. French. And then, all by himself, he translates each sentence into English. Which he could never do, word by word, if he had Parkinson's.

Unnatural Cravings

EDITH DIES. And Marvin gives, but I don't know why, to my oldest sister Judy, my mother's entire kosher—very creative—recipe collection. That Edith spends her entire life collecting. There are at least three-hundred-and-fifty different dishes. Beginning with apples and honey for the Jewish New Year. Which usually comes in September. And going all the way through summer to Tishah B'av, when Jews don't eat anything at all. We're busy fasting in commemoration of the destruction of the Second Temple. Included in Edith's collection is food appropriate to the immigrant/refugee experience. Such as coleslaw for the Fourth of July, cranberry sauce on Thanksgiving, and Wonder Bread peanut butter and jelly sandwiches with individual, little blue and yellow bags of Mike Sell's potato chips for Girl Scout overnighters. All printed in my mother's perfect handwriting. She practiced. Over and over again. Block letters. There's a particular Edith way to spread the Jiffy peanut butter. So the Wonder Bread doesn't shred.

The collection includes cuisine from all over the world. French (for Edith's family). Russian (representing Marvin's father's side). And all Jews everywhere: Ashkenazi and Sephardic. The Middle Eastern recipes—hummus, eggplant salad, chopped tomatoes, and cucumbers in *lebon* (plain white yogurt)—come much later after Edith and Marvin travel to Israel for the first time. In the early 1970s. The food is color coded on pastel, multicolored three-by-five file cards. Desserts are light green; baked, roasted, or grilled meat is pink; vegetables are yellow, fish and fowl are light blue; and all dairy dishes are printed on the original, plain white file cards. With thin red lines.

Edith's little secrets concerning exact food preparation come with each recipe. She draws circles and smiles around her favorite hints. Preheating the oven more than thirty minutes ahead of time. Greasing the pan with olive oil from Jerusalem instead of corn oil from Kansas for more flavor. Plus specific directions not to turn the salmon steaks over too soon or they'll cook unevenly. Actually, you don't *have* to turn salmon steaks. Unless you want to. Jewish American nouvelle contemporary kosher cooking is a challenge.

Only in America there are all these new food products with butter and/or milk substitutes. Talmudically speaking—in the old country—you could never butter your baked potato, load it up with sour cream, and have (your) brisket too. But today, because of modernity. It's possible. Ultimately, keeping kosher is a fiction. Not what it used to be: A deeply symbolic separation. Of Jews from the rest of the world. It's not exactly like the Jews and/or the Felmans still strictly observe the biblical dietary laws. In America, we just pretend. My mother Edith knows this. Because she does all the cooking and shopping. At Kroger's. Marvin proudly keeps kosher in the navy. Surrounded by all the *goyim*. (All his life he refuses nondairy fake butter substitutes.) His mother sends him kosher salami and rye bread. With miniature jars of Nathan's mustard tucked in newspaper in the bottom of the box. Which he passes around the barracks.

In the margins. Of her collection. Edith writes her opinion of particular dishes. Like: *good!* Or: *Excellent for Passover. Terrific Rosh Hashanah appetizer (Aunt Marge's favorite). Goes well with calf's liver and onions. Serve only in the winter. (Too hot for the summer months May–Aug.)* Occasionally my mother writes personal messages to herself. Reminders: *Add extra sugar if serving Marvin. Delete all sugar if preparing for Zeke Katz, who is diabetic. Never substitute ingredients unless the recipe says it's okay. Don't ever use butter (even though it will taste much better) instead of soybean margarine when cooking for or in a kosher household. Absolutely NO salt for Marvin's father. Jyl loves anything sweet. Jan eats most vegetables. Judy is a little more particular. . . .* The notes go on and on.

Edith has a separate filing system for everyone's taste buds. She never forgets. All our individual likes and dislikes. Especially Marvin's, and Marvin's father's. Likes and dislikes. Over the years, a small, quiet, discreet oligarchy develops. Among the Felmans. Around food preferences.

Every dish Edith ever makes is part of the collection that my father gives away. And Judy gets. To keep forever. Even the failed experiments. My father (and his father) prefer simple meals. Well done. Bland. Meat and potatoes. No sauces. Gravies. Or sautés. Which is a slight crimp to Edith's creative flare in the kitchen but she adapts wholeheartedly. Out of love. And loyalty. My oldest sister promises to make copies, to put all the recipes together in alphabetical order according to whatever Jewish holiday or American experience the food is supposed to represent. Judy swears that she'll put the finished copies in separate scrapbooks that say on the cover in bold, black block letters, "Edith's Recipes: From Honey-Glazed Carrots on *Yontif* to Baked Alaska on New Year's Eve."

Judy will then send the scrapbooks out. Fully insured/charged to Marvin. Via Federal Express. To me. Jan. Edith's sister, Aunt Shirley. And Marvin. We always eat Baked Alaska on the gentile New Year, every December thirty-first right before midnight, after eating Chinese in a booth hours earlier. Even Marvin learns to like the strawberry and chocolate ice cream tucked into a homemade-by-Edith-meringue shell and dribbled with bittersweet chocolate. Served warm. Only Judy never does make any copies. So every day, as soon as I wake up, I try hard to remember. *What are Edith's recipes?*

Honey-glazed carrots sliced julienne/French style sprinkled with extra brown sugar; fresh green beans with toasted almonds; baked-whipped-stuffed Idaho potatoes; Ohio corn-off-the-cob sautéed in onions and garlic; pot roast; brisket with raisins. (Edith's secret ingredient.) Roast, moist, golden brown Empire kosher chicken with paprika; individual capon birds stuffed with wild rice, green and purple grapes, and whole Georgia pecans. Roast Long Island duckling well done: Edith always removes the skin for crisping the first hour. Then she puts it back on. The prestripped carcass. She serves—next to the duckling—her own unique prune and pear compote. On the side. So the skin of the cooked fowl remains thoroughly crisp. Edith's ducks are kosher. Previously, they've been blessed by the *shochet*. (And ritually slaughtered.) If prunes aren't in season, Edith substitutes peaches. In her compote. Which she prefers. Anyway.

On rainy days: homemade french fries sliced extra thin; grilled Swiss cheese on dark seedless rye bread topped with chilled Vidalia onion slices. Very Russian. For appetizers on Marvin's Tuesday night bridge games with Sam Schwartz, Herb Goldman, and Russ Remick, Edith serves: Hebrew National frankfurters wrapped in Pillsbury pareve/nondairy dough with spicy mustard (kosher-style Pigs in a Blanket). The frankfurters are stuck on the ends of extra long toothpicks with red Saran Wrap twirling like miniature flags. Into the air. On Saturday afternoon, for lunch, the whole family eats pineapple and cottage cheese noodle kugel; or noodle kugel with sour cream, cherries, and chopped pecans. Whatever Edith defrosts the day before. She plans our meals weeks in advance. So she'll be ready. On the dot. For every single occasion. Current historical event. Celebration. Birthday. Or just dinner. Edith is a busy woman.

Matzo meal pancakes with homemade chunky applesauce. Made from New England Macintoshes. Not the local Red Delicious apples. From Dayton. Which aren't tart enough for Marvin. Edith's Dutch apple pie with her delicious crumbled topping; Edith's own cherry pie plus her very exhausting, labor-intensive, homemade with a full pound of butter, crisscross crust on top. Served on George Washington's Birthday. Growing up we celebrate everything. My parents want to belong. And like other Jews in Dayton (in spite of their many serious attempts), they remain completely separate from the community at large. Lincoln logs: very thin dark chocolate wafers that expand into cake when refrigerated for at least five hours. With a mocha mint whipped cream filling in between each wafer/cookie.

Edith teaches third grade at the local Jewish Day School. She teaches us and her students about dual loyalty. Edith is patriotic. An American Jew and a Jewish American. A mother of mythic proportions who dies achieving true icon status. She is presidential. One year, she bakes seven Lincoln logs and brings them to my third-grade class. I volunteer her services. Butterscotch oatmeal chocolate chip cookies. Lemon squares with powdered sugar. That Edith has to hide in a big glass jar wrapped in newspaper in the front closet. Because Judy eats an entire batch at once. Once I start to remember. The food just keeps coming. Back into my brain. Slowly at first. Then faster and faster. Until I can taste lime-green Jell-O mold overflowing with fruit cocktail and maraschino cherries. Right now. On my tongue. Lime-green Jell-O should always be served at room temperature. So it's not too cold on the tongue.

Fillet of sole lightly breaded served with fresh lemon wedges; strawberry sherbet topped with canned Dole pineapple chunks and shredded toasted coconut. Thick, well-done grilled lamb chops with dark green mint jelly; lamb shanks. And tongue. A meat delicacy. Which is very Jewish. I refuse to eat. From the inside of a cow's reddish, pink mouth. Salmon patties rolled in matzo meal whenever Marvin works late at the parking lots. We, the daughters, all hate salmon patties. With a passion that Edith ignores. Edith makes us take three bites of everything before we finish eating. And move ahead to dessert. Aunt Shirley's chocolate chiffon pie sprinkled with chopped walnut bits. We eat a lot of nuts. Because of Edith. She puts them in everything.

Sweet. Sour. Hot. Cold. Dairy. Meat. Fruit. And/or vegetable. Aunt Marge's real fudge double rich brownies.
"Aunt" Betty's mandelbrot with chocolate chips (Yid-
dish/Italian biscottis).

Chopped chicken livers served cold; fried chicken
livers served hot on Halloween. Right before we go out
as a family trick or treating. In Edith's homemade, individually designed costumes. Such as a scarecrow with a
broom stuck down and tied to Jan's back with her arms
sticking way out and straw stuffed way in; or Judy as the
mean *Wizard of Oz* witch dressed in Edith's ankle-
length black choir robe; and me. I go trick or treating
dressed as my mother's half boy/half girl. Split right
down the middle. A skirt, blouse, and lipstick on one
side; pants, suspenders and a mustache on the other.
We eat breaded veal chops sprinkled with fresh parsley.
Melon balls with orange sherbert cubes arranged beau-
tifully in a scooped out watermelon. That Edith sculpts
herself. It takes over an hour. She has to be careful. Not
to cut herself. While she scoops out the sweet pink
melon residue. With a special kitchen utensil.

*Pescado con Abramela fish with very sweet plum
sauce*, which comes to the French Jews by way of the
Northern Italian Jewish community, who didn't always
keep their milk and meat completely separate. Because
of their intense desire to eat pasta. And join with the
Italian community as a whole. Gefilte fish; chopped
eggs and chicken fat. Schmaltz from a glass jar. Henrietta Szold's stewed haddock with lemon sauce. (Hen-

rietta Szold was a famous female Jewish visionary. Not quite as daring as Emma Goldman. Henrietta founded Hadassah. The first Jewish all-women's organization. Edith becomes president of the local chapter. In Dayton. Which sends money to Israel to help pay for the multi-colored, stained-glass Chagall windows on Mount Scopus. Edith and Marvin visit the stained glass.) Edith likes to have theme meals in celebration of great historical moments. The table is decorated in crepe paper as we eat the history set down before us.

Edith loves classical music; we celebrate all the great composers' birthdays annually. (Except Wagner. Whose music until very recently is also banned in the State of Israel.) While she cooks, Edith listens: Bach's Brandenberg Concertos, Mozart's *Magic Flute* (Mozart was born in March). And Chopin's lovely, soothing Études. His B-flat Sonata for solo piano is her favorite. She serves us French pastries. Napoleons made with her own three-layer fresh strawberry and smooth yellow cream with a hint of marzipan filling. And a thin dark chocolate glaze hidden inside the second layer. We always drink mint tea with Edith's napoleons. My mother enjoys ritual. And constantly exposes her daughters to the thrill of meaningful, intentional, highly conscious acts of religious intensity.

Marvin's favorite dish is sweet and sour Moroccan *kofta*: ground lamb, beef, and veal meatballs with onions rolled in bread crumbs or matzo meal and spices. Kosher dill pickles; honey orange chicken breasts; zucchini bread with apricots; prune cake; pear kugel for extra special occasions. Flo Annon's pistachio cake made with real pistachios imported from Spain, plus one teaspoon of green food coloring and a single package of General Mills pistachio pudding. Which is very hard to find in the supermarket. In Dayton, Ohio. The finished green cake is left glistening on a big round plate dripping in Hershey's milk chocolate syrup. Baked apples in Edith's homemade pastry shells with caramel-nut-butterscotch filling. Marvin doesn't like vegetables. He's solely a meat and potato man. Like his father. Birds Eye frozen vegetables are too soft. Full of water. They lack flavor. The men eat dessert.

Once I start, Edith's food just keeps coming. Into my head. A complete and total obsession. Until I can just taste the steaming hot stuffed cabbage with ground beef, white rice, diced onions, tomatoes, and brown sugar. Coming straight into my mouth.

Edith cooks everything herself. All the time. Growing up we eat three full meals a day. Every day of the week. We, my sisters and I, "the Felman Girls," develop long, permanent, complicated, intricate, intimate relationships with all the food. That we eat. And don't eat. Left on our plates. Returned to the kitchen. I do not eat leftovers. Much later, as adolescents and fully grown adult women, we become profoundly familiar with certain forms of eating disorders. Like anorexia. Bulimia. Laxatives. And high-carbohydrate, no-protein diets. Chanukah jelly doughnuts rolled in granulated sugar.

Sufganiyot. (Edith tries to write in the Hebrew equivalent. Whenever relevant. Although she's not linguistically gifted. She does have three favorite French sayings: *Savoir faire; C'est la vie*; and *C'est la guerre*.) My mother makes everything from scratch: sweet potato *tsimmes*. The sweet potatoes are from Kentucky. Which is a border state to Ohio. Jan and Judy study French in high school. They walk around the house on Lynn Avenue saying: *Fermez la grande bouche*. Shut your big mouth. To me. Whenever we pass each other in the hallway.

Teyglach—fried dough soaked in honey; carrot cake with Philadelphia cream cheese frosting. Beet salad on Passover *and* Memorial Day. Figs stuffed with walnuts; dairy (meatless) lasagna; Star Kist tuna noodle casserole smothered in a blanket of crunchy fried onion rings from a Durkee's can with a red and blue label. And vegetable bundles that Edith always calls by their French name: *Fagots des légumes*: carrots, asparagus, white turnips with pareve margarine salted to taste and trimmed with green tips from very fresh scallions. Marvin never eats Edith's vegetable bundles. Everybody else adores the *Fagots des légumes*. Edith designs and color coordinates each plate. Before serving. Napkins and tablecloths must match. Sometimes she rearranges the seating chart. My mother loves edible flowers. Yellow and purple nasturtiums. Sitting at Edith's table is like eating Monet's garden. All his beautiful colors. And becoming slightly dizzy.

My compulsion to remember absolutely everything about Edith continues unabated. *Krimsels* at Passover: fried matzo pancakes/fritters with fruits and nuts. Prune plum upside down cake; pecan rolls individually rolled in cinnamon and white sugar. Standing rib roast and kasha *varnishkes*—buckwheat grains mixed in a bowl of bow-tie-shaped noodles. A recipe from my father's side of the family that my mother's mother, Tessie, finds too heavy. To eat. Avocados stuffed with more Philadelphia cream cheese and walnuts on Valentine's Day. When Marvin gives all his girls our own box of Esther Price chocolates, gold-foil wrapped and tied with a thick red ribbon. The French think avocados are aphrodisiacs. And so does Edith. Marvin doesn't like avocados. He prefers Esther Price. And scoops out the cream cheese and nuts. From inside Edith's avocados. Cheese blintzes for Shavuoth—the only time the Jewish people ever stand together. At the foot of Mount Sinai. Finally, after much debate, we agree to become The People of the Book.

Hamantashen with mun/poppyseed filling for Purim. We have to dress up like the characters in the Purim story: *Either* the good Queen Esther, who saves the Jewish people in Persia a long, long time ago. Today Persia is Iran. Where the Jews are still forbidden to live. *Or* Vashti, who refuses to follow the King's orders. Edith emulates Queen Esther. And longs for her daughters to do the same. We prefer Vashti. Who has a mind of her own. And reminds each of us of our Aunt

Naomi. My father's only sister. Who is banished from the kingdom of Dayton, Ohio, for not risking her life for her people. Like the good Queen Esther. Apple blintzes for Marvin's people. The last recipe in Edith's entire food collection is for crêpes suzette. My mother's mother's specialty. Which Edith files under "Z."

My sister Judy has all my mother's recipes. No one in the family ever sees them again. For twenty years Judy doesn't eat anything but baby shrimp cocktail in long-stemmed parfait dishes with spiced tomato sauce for dipping and dunking. Which isn't kosher at all. (And she knows it.)

I have no idea why Marvin gives Judy all our mother's recipes. He could have divided them equally. Among all the girls. That would have been fair. Maybe she'll start eating. Again. My father is trying to feed his oldest daughter, who is starving herself right in front of the entire family. A Jew should never go hungry. This is an embarrassment to us all. It's hard to eat in a restaurant with Judy. Who only orders baby shrimp cocktail. If anything.

I don't believe I'll ever see my mother's recipes again. I know my sister is eating Edith's recipes. One at a time. All three-hundred-and-fifty different dishes. Judy is eating Edith. Alone and in private. My sister feeds her starving self all my mother's high-cholesterol, Jewish-American-French-Russian nouvelle female kosher cuisine. I picture the whole perfect scene. Perfectly.

In her one-bedroom apartment. My sister Judy sets a beautiful table. Lights the *Shabbos* candles. Just like Edith teaches us. It takes her hours to set each place. Carefully. And with great attention to detail. First. She has to iron the ivory tablecloth. And the matching napkins. That she brings back in her large Samsonite suitcase from Dayton. After Edith dies. Next, the silverware has to be polished. Individually. Edith hates spots of any kind. She has special rags for rubbing her silver spoons back and forth. Until the family letter "F" stands out. Shining and clear. And the wine glasses. Each one has to be dusted with great care.

The water glass, which is always taller than the wine glass. Goes on the outside. According to Dear Abby, Dear Ann, and Edith Jeanne Felman. (Both Abigail van Buren and Ann Landers are from Dayton. They're Jewish girls. Identical. Twin sisters. Who don't speak to each other. But they both write advice columns for the gentiles in separate newspapers around the U.S. That Edith reads out loud. Comparing and contrasting one sister's opinion with the other.) The forks never go on top of the cloth napkin. No matter what. Even if it's cramped. Judy has a big table. The flowers are hand arranged—pink alstroemerias, cut short so eye contact is still possible.

On top of each salad plate, to the left of the fork, Judy places a single recipe. Beet salad. Avocado stuffed with Philadelphia cream cheese and walnuts. Coleslaw. There are settings for five. As if all the Felmans are coming for dinner. And Edith isn't dead yet. I have never in my entire life eaten a single meal cooked by either of my sisters. I never cook for them. Or invite them over for dinner. (Most of the time I eat alone.) For the main course, Judy has the big plates warming in the oven on low. Which is what Edith does. She's serving breaded kosher veal chops with fresh parsley; lamb shanks; pot roast; roast Long Island Duckling with Edith's own prune and pear compote; Henrietta Szold's fish stew, and *Pescado con Abramela fish with very sweet plum sauce*. After everyone is served. Judy sits down. Picks up her knife and starts to cut the recipe in the middle of her plate into bite-size pieces. She adds a little salt and freshly ground pepper. To taste. Then slowly. Very slowly. My oldest sister eats each piece of paper with Edith's perfect handwriting. She begins with Henrietta's fish stew. I picture Judy moving from place setting to place setting. Around the entire table. Taking her time. Eating the file cards as she goes. One after another. Until, she's finished. And full. We are taught to swallow completely before taking another bite. To swallow completely. And to chew with our mouths closed.

My mother's entire collection of three-hundred-and-fifty different kosher dishes from all around the world is gone. Disappears. Forever inside my oldest sister, Judy's, small stomach. I try not to be upset that I will never be able to bake Edith's green pistachio cake with real pistachios from Spain. Or her famous Lincoln logs.

It's possible to eat shredded paper slowly and not be sick. You need plenty of liquid to wash it down. Cold water. With ice cubes. Today, I hate the Jewish holidays the most. Because I can never remember how to cook anything that Edith made. I don't celebrate anymore. The food doesn't taste the same. Judy never mentions Edith's recipes again. Marvin forgets that he gives her the whole collection. Every single recipe. And all of Edith's little secrets. Her hints. With the smiles.

Jan keeps leaving me messages on my phone machine. Asking me for Edith's recipe for *Sufganiyot*. She wants to make her son jelly doughnuts for Chanukah. But there are no more doughnuts. Edith always tells us never to cry over spilled milk. So I'm not going to. Cry. Over any milk that spills. When I am growing up I drink only skim milk. Doctor's orders. I am allergic, hyper-sensitive to the real thing. I don't know what Judy does with my mother's recipes. She doesn't tell.

Private Rituals

I AM SLEEPING when my mother comes to me in a dream more vivid than when she was alive. Dressed in white silk, a sleeveless, V-neck negligee, she hovers over my bed. With her arms outstretched she reaches for me. Then, gently so as not to disturb my sleep, she lies down right beside me, wrapping her small, tight body around my own. She pulls me toward her until the round of her stomach and the curve of my back are touching. When she slips her left arm under my head, her right arm draws our bodies so close that her legs wrap completely around my legs. I am delirious in her embrace.

Lying next to my father in bed, my mother dies. Only he does not know that she is dead until four hours later. After I hear that my mother dies between 2:00 and 3:00 in the morning, I wake each morning between 2:00 and 3:00 for an entire year. I check my clock and know that my mother is dying right alongside me, in bed. I match the rhythm of my breath to the rhythm of my mother's breath so she won't die alone. In my dreams, my mother always dies in my arms.

I cannot imagine lying next to a dead person for four hours. I imagine my mother lying next to me in bed. I am a light sleeper; I feel sure I would know if she died lying right next to me. My mother slips away in the middle of the night. Later, he said they held hands. That she reached for his hand and squeezed. I do not know when this happened. Right before she fell asleep or right before she died? For almost a year, in the middle of the night, gently so as not to disturb her sleep, I reach into the darkness for my mother's hand and squeeze. Just to be sure she is still here, alive in me, I reach for her hand and squeeze. I am reaching in the dark for my mother's hand.

My mother's nurse said that her body was already cold when she undressed her for the night. And she knew as she put my mother to bed that she was dying in her arms. I picture my mother's body turning cold. My mother and I lie in bed together. I feel her body turning cold next to mine and the sudden shift in temperature in the room. When she dies my mother's body is colder than burning ice. I know. I touch her cheek with my hand. I cannot believe how cold her body is. I walk up to the casket by myself. I take my hand and touch my mother's face. I rub my fingers up and down her cheek and reach for her hand lying motionless by her side. Her skin is so cold that I have to remove my hand from hers. But as I do, a chill so severe races up my spinal cord that I open my mouth to scream. Only there is no sound. I am burning next to my mother's frozen body. But I stand next to her as long as I can. I do not want to leave, even though I am on fire, soaking in my own sweat.

When my mother dies, not a single sound leaves my lips. When I open my mouth to say the slow, mournful, ancient words that are supposed to comfort me, there is nothing. I am ashamed that I cannot say *Kaddish* for the woman who gave birth to me. During *shiva*, I cover all the mirrors and wait for the sounds that never come. In the first month of mourning, I do not go to *shul* or even pray at home. On Yom Kippur, I turn around, walk straight out of the synagogue before the davening begins. I don't come back for Yiskor. And I haven't been back since. I don't tell anyone that I cannot say *Kaddish* for my mother. It is two years since she died and still I do not understand the silence consuming me. Instead, I plant a small white pine outside my kitchen window and watch it grow each day as I slowly wash the dishes. I pour water on the dry earth beneath the tree as though I am pouring all my unshed tears back into my mother in the ground below. I imagine my tears moving slowly through the earth, making their way across the country, from the east coast to the Midwest, from daughter to mother to the Jewish cemetery I don't visit, where my mother's small frozen body is buried. When

I'm finished pouring, I pat the mulch back in place, smooth the topsoil out, and go back inside to finish washing the dishes. But I would give anything to lie down on the hard, dry ground at the base of my mother's white pine and howl into the wind for the rest of my life.

The grief lives in my body whole, not only in my throat. When it rises to the surface, just behind my eyes and right inside my mouth, I swallow, everything. Then I feel it on my skin. In the crevices of my fingers as I rub my thumb back and forth slowly in between each finger. I am holding my breath, swallowing the memories one by one until they are choking me. Only the memories live in my body, until all I am is one giant memory of mother loss. Everything reminds me of her: finely wrapped chocolate kisses and toasted pumpkin seeds; sheets of colored paper and matching envelopes— printed with my name in large black script. She is on the page in Nelly Sachs's poetry; or Hannah Senesh's parachute. While my body floats in steaming water, her spoon stirs the mint tea; she sings with Julie Andrews. I am forty, she is dead, but we are still flossing my teeth, planting olive trees in Israel at the kitchen table; eating Girl Scout cookies, and plucking all the feathers from the kosher chickens. She is Marc Chagall, Ibsen's Nora, and Emma Lazarus as we climb the Statue of Liberty and the Jefferson Memorial. She is *Charlotte's Web*, Dorothy in Oz in the school play, and Nancy Drew sitting in the car with me, backing up. She likes Eleanor

Roosevelt; adores Sarah Bernhardt; breakfast in bed and floating strawberries in fresh squeezed orange juice. She and Cherry Ames shave my legs together with their Lady Remingtons and shop for clothes I never wear. Blue jeans are forbidden. When I clip my nails,wear black mascara, use too much eye shadow, she sits on top of the toilet seat. She is in my hair when the sides are cropped really short. And she hates bikini bathing suits; pink rouge; bad breath; scented toilet paper; all body odor. She is talcum powder and Eau de London perfume; the smell of frying onions and bowling lanes. Dressed in red I hear her voice: *Red is your color, you must always wear red.*

I cannot look in the mirror without my mother looking back. I see what she sees, her eyes averted, never looking straight at me. From the time I am a little girl, I want to say out loud, *Stop, don't look away. Look at me.* But I do not say a word. *Look at me.* What is in my face that cannot hold her gaze? Her eyes live in my body, seething through my skin. When my mother dies I feel lighter than I have in years although I do not lose a pound. Now the weight is back, the weight of my mother living in me. I have to stop holding my breath and let her out. But I cannot look in a mirror without her disappointment looking back. I have my mother's eyes. Dark brown, piercing eyes that fill an entire face. I see what she sees and she knows what I see. This is the shame, locked between our eyes, that can't get out. But years before the shame there are centuries of fear.

The fear comes early. Long before I am ever born. Glasses of milk laced with terror. The terror of a whole people. That we'd be devoured, one by one. And the little girls and women are especially accessible. Because of our bodies. So wet and full and round. And dark and wide and open. That when you drink your orange juice, you gulp down the fear and swallow hard. Already, you know your daughter wouldn't fit. I am in your belly, it is very tight. I can't move around. Once I kick you really hard. We double over, caught in a spasm of excruciating pain. Me, a huge baby girl growing bigger month by month. You, a tiny woman, barely weighing in. We are always hungry, the two of us together. Our mouths open sucking. I can't get enough, floating in your yolk. You can't eat enough. Our appetites. I always want more. You always want more. You know back then I'm not going to fit. As we eat and eat and eat. Our hungry bodies never full. But I eat your fear and swallow all the bites right along with you. It seeps in everywhere. The hungry, starving fear. Of a people with no place to go and a mother. A Jewish mother with a *vilde chaye* kicking in her belly. Sometimes I can't breathe. You are holding our breath until I almost turn blue. A wild beast kicking blue in your belly. They rush us to the hospital, telling you to breathe. In and out. Slow and deep. I don't want to leave. In and out. Slow and deep. I don't ever want to leave your belly. I am born holding my breath and now I cannot let it go. It feels impossible, this breathing that I am supposed to do.

Private Rituals

You can never keep your body clean enough. Before I am born you are always washing in the sink with one leg resting on the toilet seat. And the other leg spread out, standing on the cold tile floor. What are you washing off your skin with me inside? The ancient female smells of your body giving birth? Your hands creep up between your legs, washing and scrubbing with an ugly bar of Ivory soap. You scrub so hard that my skin begins to itch. Right below the surface it begins to glow. My skin is very sensitive; I can't stand Ivory soap. I get a rash if I scrub too hard. My flesh is alive. You stand at the sink with your legs spread wide apart. You look in the mirror. When you lean over, too close to the hard porcelain sink, my head hits the ledge and I kick you really hard. Then you turn the water on, ice cold. I am freezing in your belly. Are you washing me away? Your baby *vilde chaye*, who grows wild, hemmed inside the thick, tight lining of your kosher yellow yolk?

I am floating in the water. This is what I see, lying on my back. You adoring me, the way we used to be, soaking in the tub, the round of my back and the curve of your stomach, our arms together short and strong, flapping like a pair of matching penguins splashing in the water. We are soaking and playing in the tub as you rub my back with a bar of Ivory soap and sponge it down with water from the drinking glass. You fill the bath with crystals. Blue and green like the sea, you always tell me. We make the water hot; fill the room with steam. It will always be like this you promise me, laughing in the tub. We are penguins together. I am soaking in your love of me. You never let me drown. I jump into the water, splashing all the way, and you smile just to see me splash. I always make a big splash. Only I am not splashing now. I am raging in the water, swimming hard against the current of your will.

Acknowledgments

There are certain people in my life whom I want to thank for their support as I completed this memoir.

For the unconditional love she continues to bestow upon me, I thank Linda Randall, visionary, sister, and friend.

For daring to extend the boundaries of what we all can be, I thank Pumpkin, Harry, and Sandra Lee Golvin.

I also want to thank:

Joan Featherman and Thom Herman for their infinite capacity to believe in me;

Debby King and Jo Anne Jones, who fed me and listened to endless versions of this work when they were beyond exhaustion;

Dr. Harvey Schwartz, for his wise and gentle counsel and his unique ability to reach out over the phone;

Margaret Kierstein and Bertha Josephson, who continue to inspire me with their great salmon marinade, and for their deep affection for Mrs. Esther Price, born and bred in Dayton, Ohio, and all that she represents;

Anne and Howard Irwin, who see me as an artist whether I am writing, dreaming, sleeping, or picking lettuce in the garden;

Susan Tracy for her belief in me as a writer;

Marsha Melnick, whose humor and willingness to jump over the deep end puts me in her immeasurable debt;

Julie Merberg, who is fearless;

Shulamit Reinharz, who allows me the freedom to teach in my own unique voice;

my beloved 5A students at Brandeis University, who never cease to amaze me—I hear your cheers;

Dr. Marianna Marguglio, whose patience I wore out, but without whom I would not have been able to write this book;

Martha Ackelsberg and Judith Plaskow, writers and friends who feed me all the chicken I never cook myself;

Jan, Heather, and Emily Cooper, who have to listen to my alarm going on and off!;

Arlene Murnane, who isn't afraid of a little water!;

the Five College Women's Studies Research Center, where I first began *Cravings*;

my editor, Deborah Chasman, who understands all of me—and then some;

the truest food connoisseurs I know, Clare Hemmings and Arlene Dallalfar;

Acknowledgments

Carol Denmark Felman, for her terrific sense of humor about salmon patties and for taking such wonderful care of my father;

Lauren Heidi Levin, the woman who cooks my favorite, most forbidden meal in the whole world . . . and with whom I saw my very first sea turtle swimming in the warm Caribbean Sea;

my sisters, Judy and Jan Felman, without whom there would be no "cravings" in print or in life, for their exceptional ability to appreciate my version, even though it differs dramatically from their own;

finally, my father, H. Marvin Felman, an exceptional human being and a real *mensch*, whose generous financial support has made it possible for me to live and write in the most incredible dream house imaginable. In spite of his fear of exposure, he continued to urge me on in my desire to tell "my story." This book could never have been written without my father's unending love.